ACPL ITEM
DISCARDED
P9-ELH-456

THE SERVICE FOR THE LORD'S DAY

The Worship of God

Supplemental Liturgical Resource 1

Complete Text Edition

Prepared by

The Joint Office of Worship
for the
Presbyterian Church (U.S.A.)
and the
Cumberland Presbyterian Church

Published by
The Westminster Press
Philadelphia

For Acknowledgments, see pages 190–192.

Published by The Westminster Press®
Philadelphia, Pennsylvania

PRINTED IN THE UNITED STATES OF AMERICA
4 6 8 9 7 5 3

Library of Congress Cataloging in Publication Data

Presbyterian Church (U.S.A.)
The service for the Lord's Day.

(Supplemental liturgical resource ; 1)
Includes bibliographical references.
1. Presbyterian Church (U.S.A.)—Liturgy—Texts.
2. Cumberland Presbyterian Church—Liturgy—Texts.
3. Presbyterian Church—Liturgy—Texts. I. Joint Office of Worship (U.S.) II. Cumberland Presbyterian Church.
III. Title. IV. Series: Presbyterian Church (U.S.A.) Supplemental liturgical resource ; 1.
BX8969.5.P74 1984 264'.0513 84-5220
ISBN 0-664-24643-5 (pbk.)

TABLE OF CONTENTS

PREFACE

Worship is the heart of the church's life and mission. In worship we return to the wellsprings of the faith and are engaged in communion with God who calls us. We discover new relationships of love and peace with each other and are sent to minister in the world in the name of Christ.

Worship is of primary importance to our life as the people of God. It is the principal means by which the faith is formed within us and the most visible way the faith is expressed. Because everything the church is and does flows from its worship, liturgical reform is a major concern confronting the church today. To seek the reform of worship in the light of our faith and experience is vital to the renewal of the church in our time. The primary concern involved in the reform of worship life is that our worship may have integrity and be an instrument whereby the Holy Spirit strengthens our union with Christ and engages us in ministry.

Out of this conviction, The United Presbyterian Church in the U.S.A., in its 192d General Assembly (1980), took action to begin the process to develop "a new book of services for corporate worship, including a Psalter, hymns, and other worship aids." It asked that over the "next several years a variety of worship resources be made available . . . for trial use throughout the church before any publication is finalized." It was the assembly's hope that such a book and the process leading to it "would provide a new instrument for the renewal of the church at its life-giving center."

Subsequent action by the Presbyterian Church in the U.S. and the Cumberland Presbyterian Church made those churches full partners in the project. A result of the reunion of The United Presbyterian Church in the U.S.A. and the Presbyterian Church in the U.S. is that the Presbyterian Church (U.S.A.) and the Cumberland Presbyterian Church continue as partners in the project.

This volume, *The Service for the Lord's Day,* is the first of the series to appear. It draws heavily from the two service books presently in use in the church, *The Worshipbook* and *The Book of Common Worship.* It builds upon the work of these earlier resources and includes revisions of prayers taken from them. Furthermore, it includes liturgical material drawn from the ecumenical church, as do the earlier service books, and thereby seeks to express the unity and continuity we have with Christians of every time and place.

This resource is accompanied by an abbreviated edition for the pew. The pew edition provides the congregation with what it needs to participate in the worship set forth here.

In the next few years other volumes in the series will appear, each developed to supplement *The Worshipbook* and *The Book of Common Worship.* There will be resources on Baptism, daily prayer, the psalms, Christian marriage, Christian burial, the Christian year, ordination, ministry to the sick and dying, the lectionary, and service music. When the series is completed, the material that will have appeared in the series of resources will be further revised and included in a new book of services.

In developing the resources, guidance on policy in worship is given by the Advisory Council on Discipleship and Worship. A task force of persons with expertise in the particular subject of a resource to be developed is appointed by the Joint Administrative Committee of the Joint Office of Worship. The responsibility of each task force is to prepare a manuscript on an assigned portion of the church's liturgy. The task force is to prepare liturgical text and essays that provide historical, theological, and practical background, and suggestions for using the resource. Those who served on the task force to prepare *The Service for the Lord's Day* were: Donald K. Campbell, chairperson; Horace T. Allen, Jr.; Lucile L. Hair; Cynthia A. Jarvis; David H. Pfleiderer; David W. Romig; and Harold M. Daniels, staff.

Following review by the Joint Administrative Committee, each manuscript prepared by a task force is submitted for field testing in a variety of congregations, to obtain a broad evaluation of the work. Consequently, *The Service for the Lord's Day* was widely distributed for evaluation.

Each manuscript is also carefully reviewed by the Worship Committee of the Advisory Council on Discipleship and Worship, which makes suggestions for revision. Those who serve on the Worship Committee that reviewed this manuscript were: Donald W. Stake, chairperson; Melva W. Costen; Craig D. Erickson; Frances M. Gray; Robert S. Moorhead; Franklin Perkins; J. Barrie Shepherd; Harriet Smith; Helen Wright; James G. Kirk, staff; and Elizabeth Villegas, staff.

In addition to extensive field testing and review by official bodies, suggestions for improving *The Service for the Lord's Day* were sought from liturgical scholars both in the Reformed and in other traditions. Their comments have given significant assistance.

The entire process of review and evaluation resulted in a valuable refinement of the resource. We are therefore indebted to many people who gave invaluable assistance in developing *The Service for the Lord's Day*. It is truly the work of the church and not simply the product of a small group of persons.

Following final editing, resulting from the review and field testing, the resource was again submitted to the Joint Administrative Committee of the Joint Office of Worship to be approved for publication. Those who served on this committee while *The Service for the Lord's Day* was being developed were: Melva W. Costen; Arlo D. Duba; Lucile L. Hair (former chairperson); Collier S. Harvey; James G. Kirk; Wynn McGregor; Ray Meester; Clementine Morrison; Betty Peek; David C. Partington (current chairperson); Dorothea Snyder (former chairperson); Robert Stigall; Darius L. Swann; James Vande Berg; Harold M. Daniels, staff; and Marion L. Liebert, staff.

We invite your evaluation of this resource presented to the church for trial use as it anticipates a new book of services. Send your comments to The Joint Office of Worship, 1044 Alta Vista Road, Louisville, Kentucky 40205.

We commend this volume for your use. Use it with the freedom and the flexibility intended. We pray that it will contribute to the renewal of the worship of God in your congregation.

HAROLD M. DANIELS, Director
Joint Office of Worship

ORDER FOR
THE SERVICE
FOR THE LORD'S DAY

BASIC STRUCTURE OF THE SERVICE FOR THE LORD'S DAY

ASSEMBLE IN GOD'S NAME

The people gather in the name of the Lord. Praise is offered in words of Scripture, prayer, and song. The people acknowledge their sinfulness and receive the declaration of God's forgiveness.

PROCLAIM GOD'S WORD

The Scriptures are read and their message proclaimed. Psalms, hymns, spirituals, or anthems may be sung between the readings. Responses to the proclamation of God's Word include acts of commitment and faith, the offering of concerns and prayers for local and worldwide needs, and the giving of gifts.

GIVE THANKS TO GOD

The Lord's table is prepared for the Lord's Supper.

Prayer is given in which God is praised for creation and providence, Christ's work of redemption is remembered with thanksgiving, and the Holy Spirit is invoked upon and in the church.

The bread is broken, and the bread and wine are served to the people.

GO IN GOD'S NAME

The people are sent forth with God's blessing to serve.

AN OUTLINE OF THE SERVICE FOR THE LORD'S DAY

ASSEMBLE IN GOD'S NAME

Gathering of People
Call to Worship
Hymn of Praise, Psalm, or Spiritual
Confession and Pardon
Act of Praise
The Peace

PROCLAIM GOD'S WORD

Prayer for Illumination
First Lesson
Psalm
Second Lesson
Hymn, Spiritual, or Anthem
Gospel Lesson
Sermon
Hymn or Spiritual
Creed or Affirmation of Faith
(Baptism or an Ordinance of the Church)
Prayers of Intercession
Offering

GIVE THANKS TO GOD

Preparation of the Table
Great Prayer of Thanksgiving, concluding with the Lord's Prayer
Breaking of the Bread
Communion of the People

—*Or*—

Prayer of Thanksgiving, concluding with the Lord's Prayer

GO IN GOD'S NAME

Hymn, Spiritual, or Psalm
Charge and Blessing
Going Forth

The Lord's Day: From its beginning, the Christian community has gathered on the first day of the week to hear the Scriptures read and proclaimed and to celebrate the Lord's Supper. The first day has special significance, since it marks the day Christ rose from the grave.

For early Christians, the resurrection of Jesus Christ was an event to remember and celebrate. The resurrection authenticated Jesus' ministry, defeated the power of death, and gave assurance of eternal life. Recognizing the importance of the resurrection, the New Testament community called the day of the week on which Christ rose "the Lord's day" (Rev. 1:10). It was the day to celebrate the resurrection.

The Lord's Day, the first day of the week, is therefore the very pivot of the church's calendar. In the ancient story of Creation, this day marked the beginning of creation. On the first day, God spoke light into being, separating light from darkness. In Christ's resurrection, Christians saw the beginning of the "new creation" and came to regard the day of resurrection as "the eighth day of creation." The Lord's Day is therefore a sign of God's kingdom and of hope.

ASSEMBLE IN GOD'S NAME

Worship begins with God. God takes the initiative and calls us into being. In the name of Christ we heed God's call and assemble as the community of faith.

We entered this community through Baptism. The Baptism we share in common binds us together. As we assemble about the Lord's table, all that Baptism means is renewed.

Call to Worship: A greeting from the New Testament reminds us of the One who calls us and in whose name we are assembled. Sentences from Scripture telling of God's grace remind us that worship centers on God and not on ourselves.

THE SERVICE FOR THE LORD'S DAY
with Instructions and Explanatory Notes

The order of worship (with instructions) is displayed on the right-hand pages. Explanatory notes, providing comments on the order, appear on the left-hand pages.

ASSEMBLE IN GOD'S NAME

As the people gather, one or more of the following may occur:

The people may informally greet one another.

They may prepare for worship in personal prayer or quiet meditation. 1–18*

Essential announcements may be made.

Congregational music or liturgical forms may be rehearsed.

Silence may be kept.

Music may be offered appropriate to the season or to the Scriptural texts of the day.

Call to Worship
A leader welcomes the people with a greeting based on those in the New Testament epistles. Sentences of Scripture that proclaim who God is and what God has done are spoken or read responsively. 19–25 26–51

*Numbers refer to Liturgical Texts, which begin on page 27.

Praise and Adoration: Adoration is the keynote of all true worship, of the creature before the Creator, of the redeemed before the Redeemer. In song and prayer, God is praised.

Confession of Sin: Before God's majesty and holiness we become painfully aware of our selfishness and disobedience. We repent of our sin and ask God's forgiveness. We cannot earn God's forgiveness by our repentance. Nor can we ever be worthy of God's mercy. It is only in the assurance of God's prior mercy given freely to the undeserving that we dare make our humble confession before God.

Confession of sin therefore takes us back to our baptism. In the waters of Baptism, washed in the name of the triune God, we receive God's assurance of forgiveness and cleansing. Claiming the promises of God sealed in our baptism, we boldly confess our sin and accept forgiveness. We are confident that in our dying to sin and old destructive ways, the God of boundless grace raises us to new life.

The minister declares the reality of God's forgiving mercy to all who earnestly repent and turn to God.

With joy we praise God, whose gift of grace brings the joy of forgiveness.

The Peace: In giving signs of peace to each other we express the reconciliation, unity, and love that are in Christ. The peace is a sign of the blessing and presence of God, a sharing of the peace that comes only from God. It is a glad demonstration that as God's people we are seeking to abide in the peace of God. It expresses an openness to the power of God's love to heal our brokenness and make us agents of that love in the world.

PROCLAIM GOD'S WORD

Gathered in God's name, we now open ourselves to God's life-giving Word, which comes to us through Scripture.

Readings from Scripture: We first pray that the Holy Spirit may illumine our hearts and minds so that we may hear aright and be prepared to accept God's Word for us. Readings from both the Old and the New Testament ensure that the unity and completeness of God's revelation are proclaimed.

The singing of the psalm for the day (normally after the first reading) links the readings from Old and New Testaments. Coming to us from the worship of ancient Judaism, the psalms have been at the heart of Christian prayer and praise across the centuries.

Praise and Adoration

The people respond to the promises of God's grace by singing praise in a psalm, hymn, or spiritual An opening prayer of adoration, or the PRAYER FOR THE DAY,⁺ may be said. 52–63

Confession of Sin⁺

The people are called to confession with a sentence of Scripture that promises God's forgiveness. 64–73

The people confess their sin, using a prayer, a penitential psalm, or appropriate music. 74–82

A period of silence may be observed before, within, or following the prayer of confession.

Music of a penitential character may follow the prayer. 83–86

Assurance of God's forgiving grace is declared by the minister. 87–91

A joyful response is sung or said. 92–97

The people may exchange THE PEACE⁺ by offering one another signs of reconciliation. 98–100

PROCLAIM GOD'S WORD

Readings from Scripture

A PRAYER FOR ILLUMINATION or the PRAYER FOR THE DAY⁺ 101–111

It is appropriate that the lessons from Scripture be those suggested in a lectionary; they may include three lessons: Old Testament, Epistle, and Gospel. Between the 112–118

⁺Denotes alternate location is possible. See page 26.

The Sermon: The God who speaks in Scripture speaks to us now. The God who acted in Biblical history acts today. Rooted in Scripture, faithful preaching confronts us with the liberating Word and witnesses to God's continuing activity among us and in the life of the world.

Response to the Word: The proclamation of God's Word in readings from Scripture and sermon invites a response of faith. We respond in song, confession of faith, prayer, and offering.

A hymn is sung. The hymn may be related to the theme of the day or lead to the prayer, or to a baptism or an ordinance that might follow.

We express our faith by a creed. The Nicene Creed and the Apostles' Creed express the faith tradition of the whole church, the faith into which we were baptized. The creed is our "pledge of allegiance," a reaffirmation of our desire to live and die in the faith. The creed thus renews the profession of faith made in our baptism.

Baptism, commissioning (confirmation), reception of members, or an ordinance of the church follows the proclamation as the obedient response binding us to the fellowship of the church.

Prayers of Intercession: In response to God's Word we offer our intercessions. Across the ages the church in its worship has prayed for the church universal, the world, all in authority, and those in distress or need. At no other time in its worship is the community of faith more conscious of the needs of the life of the world. We pray for the world because God loves the world. God created it and cares for it. God sent Jesus, who died for it. God is working to lead it toward the future God has for it. To abide in God's love is to share God's concern for the world. Our prayers should therefore be as wide as God's love and as specific as God's tender compassion for the least ones among us.

An Offering: Having prayed for the world, we put ourselves where our prayers are. In grateful response for the abundance of God's grace, we offer

lessons, the PSALM FOR THE DAY, hymns, spirituals, or anthems related to the texts may be included.

The Sermon
When the Bible has been read, its message is proclaimed in a sermon or other exposition of God's Word. An ASCRIPTION OF PRAISE may conclude the sermon. 119–126

Response to the Word
After the sermon, an INVITATION may be given to any who wish to make or renew personal commitment to Christ and his kingdom. 127–134

A HYMN or other music related to the preceding proclamation, or to what is to follow, may be sung. If Baptism (or an ordinance of the church) follows, candidates may be presented during the singing of the hymn.

(*CONFESSION OF SIN, WORDS OF PARDON, and THE PEACE) 64–100

The people may say or sing a CREED of the church or an affirmation of faith drawn from Scripture. When Baptism is celebrated, the Apostles' Creed is said if it is not used in the baptismal rite. 135–143

When BAPTISM (or an ORDINANCE of the church) is celebrated, it is appropriately included here.

Prayers of Intercession
The people may express concerns for prayer. Prayers for worldwide and local concerns are offered. 144–166

An Offering
Silence or appropriate music may accompany the 167–179

ourselves to be instruments of God's peace, love, and justice. As stewards we give from what God has given us, acknowledging that the world is not ours but God's.

GIVE THANKS TO GOD

From New Testament times the celebration of the Lord's Supper on each Lord's Day has been the norm of Christian worship. Nevertheless, most Protestant congregations are not yet able to celebrate weekly. The structure of this order is therefore designed to accommodate those Sundays when the Eucharist is not included. When the Sacrament is not celebrated, all components of the order for worship are included and follow the same sequence as on sacramental occasions. Only that which pertains exclusively to the Sacrament is deleted. The parallel structure thus reminds us that the norm of all Lord's Day worship is a service in which the Scriptures are read and interpreted and the Lord's Supper is celebrated.

Preparation of the Table: If the Eucharist is to be celebrated, the minister and elders take the bread and wine and prepare the table.

Holy Communion was given us by Christ himself. Before church governments were devised, before creeds were formalized, even before the first word of the New Testament was written, the Lord's Supper was firmly fixed at the heart of Christian faith and life. From the church's inception, Lord's Day and Lord's Supper were joined. Worship on each Lord's Day was a service of Word and Sacrament.

With bread and wine, in words and actions, the promises of God are made visible and concrete. The Word we have heard read and preached is now confirmed, for all that the life, death, and resurrection of Christ means is focused in this Sacrament.

Invitation to the Table: Through the waters of baptism, we are born into Christ's family. That family is nourished and sustained at this table. Therefore, all who are baptized and being nurtured in the faith of Jesus Christ are invited to come to this table. We are invited to come, humbly trusting God's mercy, rejoicing in all God has done for us. Though we are baptized but once, the Eucharist renews everything for which our baptism was the sign and seal.

The Lord's Supper is more than a recalling of events of long ago. In the Sacrament we participate now in all that God's coming in Christ means. The power and presence of Christ is a reality in this gathering at his table. We are joined anew to him who is the source of life.

gathering of the people's offerings. As the gifts are brought forward, a doxology, spiritual, or hymn of praise is sung.

GIVE THANKS TO GOD

It is fitting that the Lord's Supper be celebrated as often as each Lord's Day. When it is celebrated, the service proceeds as follows:

When the Lord's Supper is not celebrated, the service continues with a Prayer of Thanksgiving:

Preparation of the Table
The minister(s) and elders prepare the table with bread and wine during the gathering of the gifts. The bread and wine may be brought to the table, or uncovered if already in place.

Invitation to the Table
The minister invites the people to the Sacrament using words from Scripture.

180–182

The Great Prayer of Thanksgiving: The table having been set, the minister prays the blessing, giving thanks over the bread and wine. In joyful expectation, we join first in a dialogue which Christians have used for centuries when gathering at the Lord's table.

As the people of God, we praise God for all God's mighty acts in past, present, and future, in the manner of the Jewish blessings from which the prayer derives. We praise God for creating all things, for establishing the covenant, for giving the law and sending prophets, for showing boundless love and mercy, and for the particular act of God that is being celebrated.

Then in one voice, with choirs of angels and with the faithful of every time and place, we adore the triune God. The "Holy, holy, holy Lord," the song of the heavenly hosts, eternally being sung before God's majesty (Isa. 6:1–5; Rev. 4:8), is joined with the chants of praise that greeted Jesus' entry into Jerusalem (Ps. 118:26; Matt. 21:9).

As the great thanksgiving continues, we rejoice most especially in God's coming to us in Jesus Christ, who lived, suffered, and died for us, rose from the grave, and will come again to claim his kingdom. In remembering the words and actions of Jesus in the upper room, we are assured of the fulfillment of his promise to be among us in the eating and drinking of this bread and wine. And so we joyfully acclaim Christ who died, is risen, and will come again.

The Holy Spirit is then invoked, to the end that this celebration may be for us all that Christ wills this Sacrament to be. We pray that the life-giving Spirit may renew in us all of the benefits of Christ's redemption, rekindle among us the unity we have in Christ, empower us to do Christ's work in the world, and lead us to the glory of God's eternal kingdom.

The prayer concludes in a climax of praise to the triune God. Together we shout the great *"Amen!"*

On Sundays when the Lord's Supper is not celebrated, a nonsacramental prayer of thanksgiving, similar in structure, is prayed.

The Great Prayer of Thanksgiving 183–196

The minister introduces this prayer using the following dialogue, which may be said or sung:

The Lord be with you.

And also with you.

Lift up your hearts.

We lift them to the Lord.

Let us give thanks to the Lord our God.

It is right to give our thanks and praise.

The minister then leads the people in the great thanksgiving. The prayers provided are patterned according to this outline:

Praise is given to God for creation and providence.

Christ's work of redemption and his gift of the Sacrament are remembered with thanks.

The action of the Holy Spirit is sought.

At the conclusion of the prayer, the people respond:

Amen.

The Prayer of Thanksgiving 197–203

A leader introduces this prayer using the following dialogue, which may be said or sung:

The Lord be with you.

And also with you.

Lift up your hearts.

We lift them to the Lord.

Let us give thanks to the Lord our God.

It is right to give our thanks and praise.

The people are then led in a prayer of thanks. The prayers provided are patterned according to this outline:

Praise is given to God for creation, providence, and the blessings of this life.

Christ's work of redemption is remembered with thanks.

Thanksgiving is expressed for the gifts of the Holy Spirit.

At the conclusion of the prayer, the people respond:

Amen.

The Lord's Prayer: Made one in Christ, we now pray the family prayer of the people of God.

Breaking of the Bread: The bread is broken for serving. The apostle Paul saw in the sharing of one loaf and one cup a symbol of our oneness in Christ.

Communion of the People: We come to the table of the Lord trusting in God's love and mercy, confident that in eating this bread and drinking this cup we abide in Christ and he in us.

Holy Communion is both a personal and a communal experience. The Sacrament is for each person, but we gather at the Lord's table not simply as individuals. We come to the table as members together of God's family, the body of Christ, the church. The Lord's Supper is the family meal of the people of God.

In the Eucharist, not only do we participate in the salvation events from the past, but we participate in God's future as well. This Sacrament is a glad resurrection feast, an anticipation of the great Banquet of the New Age, of the coming of the kingdom of God. We see what we ought to be, the holy community, the pledge of creation's destiny, the world as God wills it. We are thus given a foretaste of the goal of all the ages, when every creature of heaven and earth will acclaim Jesus Christ as Lord.

GO IN GOD'S NAME

The God who calls us together in worship now sends us forth in service.

Praise: We praise God for Christ's presence with us in Word and Sacrament, and we claim the strength and guidance of the Holy Spirit as we move out in ministry.

Charge: We are commissioned to obedient and grateful ministry as God's agents to heal life's brokenness. By the power of the Spirit let us be what Christ has redeemed us to be.

Blessing: The blessing of the triune God is given. Assured of God's peace and blessing, we are confident that God goes with us to our tasks.

The Lord's Prayer	204–208	**The Lord's Prayer**	204–208
Breaking of the Bread The minister breaks a loaf of bread in full view of the people.			209–211
Communion of the People During the serving of the Sacrament, psalms, spirituals, gospel songs, or hymns may be sung, or silence kept.			212–213 214–218
After all are served, a prayer may be offered.			219–229

GO IN GOD'S NAME

Praise
A hymn of praise, spiritual, or psalm is sung.

Charge
In the words of Scripture the congregation is charged to go forth to minister in the name of Christ. 230–239

Blessing
The minister gives God's blessing to the congregation, using a Scriptural benediction. 240–245

Personal prayer or meditation may follow. 246–247

Instrumental music is appropriate.

*Alternate Locations of Certain Elements of Worship

CONFESSION OF SIN and WORDS OF PARDON, when not included at the beginning of the service following PRAISE AND ADORATION, may be located at either of these alternative places:

1. Following the sermon as a RESPONSE TO THE WORD (after the HYMN or before BAPTISM or an ORDINANCE).
2. Following the PRAYERS OF INTERCESSION.

In no case should confession be included more than once in the course of the service.

THE PRAYER FOR THE DAY (see *The Worshipbook,* pages 135–163) may be included in PRAISE AND ADORATION at the beginning of the service, or may immediately precede the READINGS FROM SCRIPTURE.

THE PEACE, when not exchanged following the WORDS OF PARDON, may be located at other places such as:

1. Before the offering.
2. Following the Lord's Prayer.
3. Following Communion of the people, or (on non-Communion Sundays) following the charge and blessing.

LITURGICAL TEXTS

PRAYERS FOR USE BEFORE THE SERVICE 1–18

The following prayers may be used by worshipers for personal prayer before the service begins.

1

Eternal God,
you have called us to be members of one body.
Join us with those
who in all times and places have praised your name;
that, with one heart and mind,
we may show the unity of your church,
and bring honor to our Lord and Savior,
Jesus Christ. Amen.

2

Everlasting God,
in whom we live and move and have our being:
You have made us for yourself,
so that our hearts are restless
until they rest in you.
Give us purity of heart
and strength of purpose,
that no selfish passion may hinder us from knowing your will,
no weakness keep us from doing it;
that in your light we may see light clearly,
and in your service find perfect freedom;
through Jesus Christ our Lord. Amen.

3

Almighty God,
you pour out the spirit of grace and supplication
on all who desire it.
Deliver us from cold hearts and wandering thoughts,
that with steady minds and burning zeal
we may worship you
in spirit and in truth;
through Jesus Christ our Lord. Amen.

4

God of grace,
you have given us minds to know you,
hearts to love you,
and voices to sing your praise.
Fill us with your Spirit,
that we may celebrate your glory
and truly worship you;
through Jesus Christ our Lord. Amen.

5

O Lord our God,
you are always more ready to bestow your good gifts upon us
than we are to seek them.
You are more willing to give
than we desire or deserve.
Help us so to seek that we may truly find,
so to ask that we may joyfully receive,
so to knock that the door of your mercy may be opened for us;
through Jesus Christ our Lord. Amen.

6

Almighty God, you built your church
upon the foundation of the apostles and prophets,
with Jesus Christ himself as the cornerstone.
Join us together by their teaching,
so that we may be a holy temple
in whom your Spirit dwells;
through Jesus Christ our Lord. Amen.

7

Almighty God, we pray for your blessing
on the church in this place.
Here may the faithful find salvation,
and the careless be awakened.
Here may the doubting find faith,
and the anxious be encouraged.
Here may the tempted find help,
and the sorrowful comfort.
Here may the weary find rest,
and the strong be renewed.

Here may the aged find consolation,
and the young be inspired;
through Jesus Christ our Lord. Amen.

8

O God,
light of the minds that know you,
life of the souls that love you,
strength of the thoughts that seek you:
help us so to know you
that we may truly love you,
so to love you
that we may fully serve you,
whose service is perfect freedom;
through Jesus Christ our Lord. Amen.

9

Bless us, O God,
with a reverent sense of your presence,
that we may be at peace
and may worship you with all our mind and spirit;
through Jesus Christ our Lord. Amen.

10

Before Holy Communion

O Jesus, our great high priest,
be present with us as you were present with your disciples,
and make yourself known to us in the breaking of bread. Amen.

11

Before Holy Communion

We do not presume to come to your table,
O merciful Lord,
trusting in our own goodness,
but in your all-embracing love and mercy.
We are not worthy even to gather up the crumbs under your table,
but it is your nature always to have mercy.
Grant therefore that, as we eat the body of your Son,
and drink his blood,
we may always remain in him and he in us. Amen.

One of the following prayers may be used with the choir:

12
Serve the Lord with gladness,

Come before the presence of the Lord with singing. *Ps. 100:1*

O God,
the angels of heaven proclaim your glory without ceasing.
Help us as we serve you in your house,
that in psalms and hymns and spiritual songs
we may sing to you with our whole heart;
through Jesus Christ our Lord.

Amen.

13
Praise the Lord.

The Lord's name be praised.

Great God,
you have been generous
and marvelously kind.
Give us such wonder, love, and gratitude
that we may sing praises to you
and joyfully honor your name;
through Jesus Christ our Lord.

Amen.

14
O Lord, open our lips,

And our mouth shall proclaim your praise.

God of glory,
God of grace,
before whose face our vision fails,
help us to sing your praise gladly,
and to worship you in spirit and in truth;
through Jesus Christ our Lord.

Amen.

When elders meet before worship, they may wish to use one of the following prayers:

15

Ever-present God,
without your Word we have nothing to say.
Without your Spirit we are helpless.
Give us your Holy Spirit,
that we may lead your people in prayer,
proclaim the good news,
and gratefully praise your name;
through Jesus Christ our Lord.

Amen.

16

Startle us, O God, with your truth,
and open our minds to your Spirit;
that we may be one with Christ our Lord,
and serve as faithful disciples,
through Jesus Christ.

Amen.

17

Before Holy Communion

Almighty God,
you have set a table before us,
and called us to feast with you.
Prepare us in mind and spirit
to minister in your name,
and to honor your Son, our Lord, Jesus Christ.

Amen.

18

In preparation for worship, the people may wish to meditate upon the law of God.

THE LAW OF GOD

God spoke all these words, saying,
I am the Lord your God.

You shall have no other gods before me.

You shall not make for yourself a graven image,
or any likeness of anything that is in heaven above,
or that is in the earth beneath,
or that is in the water under the earth;
you shall not bow down to them or serve them.

You shall not take the name of the Lord your God in vain.

Remember the Sabbath day, to keep it holy.

Honor your father and your mother.

You shall not kill.

You shall not commit adultery.

You shall not steal.

You shall not bear false witness against your neighbor.

You shall not covet your neighbor's house;
you shall not covet your neighbor's wife,
or anything that is your neighbor's. *Ex. 20:1–17*

SUMMARY OF THE LAW

Our Lord Jesus said:

You shall love the Lord your God
with all your heart,
and with all your soul,
and with all your mind.
This is the great and first commandment.
And the second is like it,
You shall love your neighbor as yourself.
On these two commandments
depend all the law and the prophets. *Matt. 22:37–40*

WORDS OF GREETING 19–25

19
The Lord be with you.

And also with you.

Ruth 2:4

20
The grace of the Lord Jesus Christ
be with you all.

II Thess. 3:18

And also with you.

21
The grace of our Lord Jesus Christ,
the love of God,
and the communion of the Holy Spirit
be with you all.

II Cor. 13:14

And also with you.

22
Grace to you and peace
from God our Father
and the Lord Jesus Christ.

Rom. 1:7 and elsewhere

23
Grace, mercy, and peace
from God the Father
and Christ Jesus our Lord.

I Tim. 1:2
II Tim. 1:2

24
Grace and peace be yours in fullest measure,
through the knowledge of God
and Jesus our Lord.

II Peter 1:2

25
Grace be to you and peace,
from God who is and who was
and who is to come,
and from Jesus Christ, the faithful witness,
the firstborn from the dead
and ruler of the monarchs of the earth.

Rev. 1:4, 5

SENTENCES OF SCRIPTURE **26–51**

One or more of the following may be used.

26
Praise the Lord.

The Lord's name be praised.

27
Christ is risen.

The Lord is risen. Alleluia. *Luke 24:34*

28
Our help is in the name of the Lord,

who made heaven and earth. *Ps. 124:8*

29
Alleluia.
Christ our Passover is sacrificed for us;

Therefore let us keep the feast.
Alleluia. *I Cor. 5:7, 8*

(During Lent the Alleluia is traditionally omitted.)

30
What shall we render to the Lord
for all the Lord's bounty to us?

We will lift up the cup of salvation
and call on the name of the Lord. *Ps. 116:12, 13*

31
Taste and see that the Lord is good.

Happy are they who find refuge in God. *Ps. 34:8*

32
This is the day the Lord has made;

let us rejoice and be glad in it. *Ps. 118:24*

33
O magnify the Lord with me,

let us exalt the name of the Lord together. *Ps. 34:3*

34
Give thanks to the Lord,
for the Lord is good.

God's love endures forever. *Ps. 106:1 and elsewhere*

35
O come, let us sing to the Lord

and shout with joy to the rock of our salvation!

Let us come into God's presence with thanksgiving,

singing joyful songs of praise. *Ps. 95:1, 2*

36
The earth and all it contains belong to the Lord,

The world and those who live in it. *Ps. 24:1*

37
They who wait upon the Lord
shall renew their strength.

They shall mount up with wings as eagles,

They shall run and not be weary,

They shall walk and not faint. *Isa. 40:31*

38
Make a joyful noise to the Lord, all the lands!

Serve the Lord with gladness!

Come into God's presence with singing!

Enter the courts of the Lord with praise! *Ps. 100:1, 2, 4*

39
Clap your hands, all peoples!

Shout to God with songs of joy. *Ps. 47:1*

40
Blessed be the God and Father of our Lord Jesus Christ!
By the great mercy of God
we have been born anew to a living hope
through the resurrection of Jesus Christ from the dead. *I Peter 1:3*

Alleluia.

41
In the name of the Father,
and of the Son,
and of the Holy Spirit. *Matt. 28:19*

Amen.

42
In the beginning was the Word,
and the Word was with God,
and the Word was God. *John 1:1*

43
God's love has been poured into our hearts
through the Holy Spirit
which has been given to us. *Rom. 5:5*

44
Thus says the high and exalted One,
whose name is Holy, who lives forever:
"I dwell in a high and holy place,
but I also live
with those who are broken and humble in spirit,
to revive the spirit of the humble,
to restore the courage of the broken." *Isa. 57:15*

45
God is our refuge and strength,
a present help in trouble.
Therefore we will not fear
though the earth should change,
though the mountains shake in the heart of the sea;
though its waters roar and foam,
though the mountains tremble with its tumult. *Ps. 46:1–3*

46
God is spirit,
and those who worship God
must worship in spirit and truth. *John 4:24*

47
I appeal to you, brothers and sisters,
by the mercies of God,
to present your bodies as a living sacrifice,
holy and acceptable to God.
This is your spiritual worship. *Rom. 12:1*

48
God sent the Son into the world
not to condemn the world,
but that the world might be saved through him. *John 3:17*

49
Beloved, let us love one another, for love is of God.
All who love are born of God and know God.
All who do not love do not know God,
for God is love. *I John 4:7, 8*

50
From the rising of the sun to its setting
my name is great among the nations,
says the Lord of hosts. *Mal. 1:11*

51
Day and night around the throne they never stop singing:
"Holy, holy, holy, is the Lord God Almighty,
who was, who is, and who is to come." *Rev. 4:8*

The psalm for the day, suggested in the lectionary, may include verses appropriate for the opening of worship. Other sentences from Scripture that may be used include:

Ps. 95:6, 7
Ps. 96:1–3
Ps. 96:2–4a
Ps. 100:2, 4, 5
Ps. 100:3
Titus 3:4–8
Heb. 1:1–3
Heb. 4:14, 16
II Peter 1:2–4
I John 4:9

*The prayer for the day (*The Worshipbook, *pages 135–163) may be used rather than the opening prayers provided here, thereby enabling a prayer for illumination to be used before the readings from Scripture.*

52

Almighty God,
to whom all hearts are open,
all desires known,
and from whom no secrets are hid:
cleanse the thoughts of our hearts
by the inspiration of your Holy Spirit,
that we may perfectly love you
and worthily magnify your holy name;
through Christ our Lord.

Amen

53

God of all glory,
on this first day
you began creation,
bringing light out of darkness.
On this first day
you began your new creation,
raising Jesus Christ out of the darkness of death.
On this Lord's day
grant that we,
the people you create by water and the Spirit,
may be joined with all your works
in praising you for your great glory.
Through Jesus Christ,
in union with the Holy Spirit,
we praise you now and forever.

Amen.

54
Eternal God, Lord of heaven and earth,
we praise you for your greatness.
Your wisdom is seen in all your works.
Your grace and truth are revealed
in Jesus Christ your Son.
Your power and presence are given us
through your Holy Spirit.
Therefore we revere your holy name,
O blessed Trinity, for ever and ever.

Amen.

55
O God, you are infinite,
eternal and unchangeable,
glorious in holiness,
full of love and compassion,
abundant in grace and truth.
All your works praise you
in all places of your dominion,
and your glory is revealed
in Jesus Christ our Savior.
Therefore we praise you,
blessed and holy Trinity,
one God, for ever and ever.

Amen.

56
O God, light of the hearts that see you,
life of the souls that love you,
strength of the thoughts that seek you:
to turn from you is to fall,
to turn to you is to rise,
to abide in you is to stand fast forever.
Although we are unworthy to approach you,
or to ask anything at all of you,
grant us your grace and blessing
for the sake of Jesus Christ our Redeemer.

Amen.

57

You are holy,
O Lord, our Creator and Father,
giving us mercies beyond number.
You are holy,
O Savior Jesus Christ,
loving and setting us free.
You are holy,
O Spirit of truth and peace,
leading us in ways that are right.
O holy, eternal Trinity,
we praise you for ever and ever.

Amen.

58

Almighty God,
you raised Jesus from the grave
and opened the way to eternal life.
We praise you
that you are a God who is free to act,
strong to redeem,
and loving in all your ways;
through Jesus Christ our Savior.

Amen.

59

God of light and truth,
you are beyond our grasp or conceiving.
Before the brightness of your presence
the angels veil their faces.
With lowly reverence and adoring love
we acclaim your glory
and sing your praise,
for you have shown us your truth and love
in Jesus Christ our Savior.

Amen.

60
O God,
source of all beauty and goodness,
your grace comes fresh every morning.
In each new day you give us light.
We praise you for your never-failing love
that satisfies our needs
and shows us the way to follow.
We rejoice in your constant care,
for you are faithful in love for all people,
offering your salvation through Jesus Christ.

Amen.

61
God of eternity,
before you lips are silenced in awe and wonder.
Mere words fail to praise
the fullness of your Word for us
spoken in Jesus Christ.
Let our lives reflect his love
and so return to you all praise and glory
by all we say and do.

Amen.

62
God of Abraham and Ruth,
you call us to embark on a journey of faith.
We stand before you,
ready to hear your call
and to follow where you lead,
for you have claimed us by your mercy
and set before us eternal promises in Jesus Christ,
with whom we live to give you all glory
in the power of the Holy Spirit.

Amen.

63

In peace, let us pray to the Lord.

Lord, have mercy.

For the peace from above, and for our salvation,
let us pray to the Lord.

Lord, have mercy.

For the peace of the whole world,
for the well-being of the church of God,
and for the unity of all,
let us pray to the Lord.

Lord, have mercy.

For this house of prayer,
and for all who offer here their worship and praise,
let us pray to the Lord.

Lord, have mercy.

Help, save, comfort, and defend us, gracious Lord.

Amen.

INVITATIONS TO CONFESSION OF SIN 64–73

64

If we claim that we have no sin,
we deceive ourselves,
and the truth is not in us.
But if we confess our sins,
God who is faithful and just
will forgive our sins
and cleanse us from all unrighteousness. *I John 1:8, 9*

Let us confess our sins
against God and our neighbor.

65

The proof of God's amazing love is this:
while we were sinners
Christ died for us.
Because we have faith in him, *Rom. 5:8*
we dare to approach God with confidence. *Heb. 4:16*

Let us admit our sins before God.

66

Since we have a great high priest
who has passed through the heavens,
Jesus, the Son of God,
let us with confidence
draw near to the throne of grace,
that we may receive mercy
and find grace to help us in time of need. *Heb. 4:14, 16*

Let us ask God to forgive us.

67

If anyone sins,
we have someone who pleads with the Father
on our behalf—
Jesus Christ, the righteous one.
And Christ himself is the means
by which our sins are forgiven,

74

Merciful God,
we confess that we have sinned against you
in thought, word, and deed.
We have not loved you
with our whole heart and mind and strength;
we have not loved our neighbors as ourselves.
In your mercy forgive what we have been,
help us amend what we are,
and direct what we shall be,
so that we may delight in your will
and walk in your ways,
to the glory of your holy name. Amen.

75

Eternal God, our judge and redeemer,
we confess that we have tried to hide from you,
for we have done wrong.
We have lived for ourselves,
and turned from our neighbors.
We have refused to bear the troubles of others.
We have ignored the pain of the world,
and passed by the hungry, the poor, and the oppressed.

O God,
in your great mercy forgive our sin
and free us from selfishness,
that we may choose your will
and obey your commandments;
through Jesus Christ our Savior. Amen.

76

Merciful God,
we confess that we have often failed
to be an obedient church.
We have not done your will,
we have broken your law,
we have rebelled against your love.
We have not loved our neighbors,
and have refused to hear the cry of the needy.

Forgive us, we pray,
and free us for joyful obedience;
through Jesus Christ our Lord. Amen.

77
Eternal God,
in whom we live and move and have our being,
your face is hidden from us by our sins,
and we forget your mercy in the blindness of our hearts.
Cleanse us from all our offenses,
and deliver us from proud thoughts and vain desires.
With lowliness and meekness
may we draw near to you,
confessing our faults,
confiding in your grace,
and finding in you our refuge and strength;
through Jesus Christ your Son. Amen.

Silent confession may follow.

78
Almighty God,
in Jesus Christ you called us
to be a servant people,
but we do not do what you command.
We are often silent when we should speak,
and useless when we could be useful.

Have mercy on us, O God.
Forgive us and free us from sin;
through Jesus Christ our Lord. Amen.

79
Almighty and merciful God,
we have erred and strayed from your ways like lost sheep.
We have followed too much
the devices and desires of our own hearts.
We have offended against your holy laws.
We have left undone those things which we ought to have done;
and we have done those things which we ought not to have done.

O Lord, have mercy upon us.
Spare those who confess their faults.
Restore those who are penitent,
according to your promises declared to the world
in Christ Jesus our Lord.
And grant, O merciful God, for his sake,
that we may live a holy, just, and humble life
for the glory of your holy name. Amen.

80

Almighty God,
you love us, but we do not love you fully.
You call, but we do not always listen.
We often walk away from neighbors in need,
wrapped in our own concerns.
We often condone evil, hatred, warfare, and greed.

God of grace,
help us to admit our sin,
so that as you move toward us in mercy,
we may repent, turn to you, and receive forgiveness;
through Jesus Christ our Redeemer. Amen.

81

Merciful God,
you pardon all who truly repent and turn to you.
We humbly confess our sins and ask your mercy.
We have not loved you with a pure heart,
nor have we loved our neighbor as ourselves.
We have not done justice, loved kindness,
or walked humbly with you, our God.

Have mercy on us, O God, in your loving-kindness.
In your great compassion,
cleanse us from our sin.
Create in us a clean heart, O God,
and renew a right spirit within us.
Do not cast us from your presence,
or take your Holy Spirit from us.
Restore to us the joy of your salvation
and sustain us with your bountiful Spirit. Amen.

82

**Holy and merciful God,
in your presence we confess
our sinfulness, our shortcomings,
and our offenses against you.
You alone know how often we have sinned
in wandering from your ways,
in wasting your gifts,
in forgetting your love.**

**Have mercy on us, O Lord,
for we are ashamed and sorry
for all we have done to displease you.
Forgive our sins,
and help us to live in your light,
and walk in your ways,
for the sake of Jesus Christ our Savior. Amen.**

The "Lord, have mercy" may be said or sung using one of the following forms. Much of the available music is penitential in nature. If such music is used, it is appropriate that the "Lord, have mercy" be placed after the confession of sin and silent prayer, and before the declaration of pardon.

83

Lord, have mercy.
Christ, have mercy.
Lord, have mercy.

84

Lord, have mercy.
Lord, have mercy.

Christ, have mercy.
Christ, have mercy.

Lord, have mercy.
Lord, have mercy.

85

Lord, have mercy on us.
Lord, have mercy on us.
Lord, have mercy on us.

Christ, have mercy on us.
Christ, have mercy on us.
Christ, have mercy on us.

Lord, have mercy on us.
Lord, have mercy on us.
Lord, have mercy on us.

86

Kyrie eleison.
Christe eleison.
Kyrie eleison.

87
The mercy of the Lord
is from everlasting to everlasting.
I declare to you, in the name of Jesus Christ,
you are forgiven.

May the God of mercy,
who forgives you all your sins,
strengthen you in all goodness,
and by the power of the Holy Spirit
keep you in eternal life.

Amen.

88
The mercy of the Lord
is from everlasting to everlasting.
I declare to you, in the name of Jesus Christ,
we are forgiven.

May the God of mercy,
who forgives us all our sins,
strengthen us in all goodness,
and by the power of the Holy Spirit
keep us in eternal life.

Amen.

89
Hear the good news!

The saying is sure and worthy of full acceptance,
that Christ Jesus came into the world to save sinners. *I Tim. 1:15*

He himself bore our sins
in his body on the cross,
that we might be dead to sin
and be alive to all that is good. *I Peter 2:24*

In the name of Jesus Christ,
you (we) are forgiven.

Glory to God. Amen.

90

Hear the good news!

Who is in a position to condemn?
Only Christ,
and Christ died for us,
Christ rose for us,
Christ reigns in power for us,
Christ prays for us. *Rom. 8:34*

Anyone who is in Christ
is a new creation.
The old life has gone;
a new life has begun. *II Cor. 5:17*

Friends,
believe the gospel.

In Jesus Christ, we are forgiven.

91

Hear the good news!

If we have died with Christ,
we believe that we shall also live with him.
So you also must consider yourselves dead to sin
and alive to God in Christ Jesus. *Rom. 6:8, 11*

Friends,
believe the good news.

In Jesus Christ, we are forgiven.

92

Glory to God in the highest,
and peace to God's people on earth.

Lord God, heavenly King,
almighty God and Father,
we worship you, we give you thanks,
we praise you for your glory.

Lord Jesus Christ, only Son of the Father,
Lord God, Lamb of God,
You take away the sin of the world:
have mercy on us;
You are seated at the right hand of the Father:
receive our prayer.

For you alone are the Holy One,
you alone are the Lord,
you alone are the Most High,
Jesus Christ,
with the Holy Spirit,
in the glory of God the Father. Amen.

93

Holy God,
Holy and Mighty,
Holy Immortal One,

Have mercy upon us.

94

You are the Lord, giver of mercy!
You are the Christ, giver of mercy!
You are the Lord, giver of mercy!

95

Worthy is Christ, the Lamb who was slain,
whose blood set us free to be people of God.
Power and riches and wisdom and strength,
and honor and blessing and glory are his.

This is the feast of victory for our God.

Sing with all the people of God
and join in the hymn of all creation:
Blessing and honor and glory and might
be to God and the Lamb forever. Amen.

This is the feast of victory for our God,
for the Lamb who was slain has begun his reign.
Alleluia. Alleluia.

Rev. 5:12, 9, 13
7:10, 12
19:4, 6–9

96

You are full of compassion and mercy, O Lord,
slow to anger and of great kindness.

You have not dealt with us according to our sins,
nor rewarded us according to our wickedness.

For as the heavens are high above the earth,
so is your mercy great upon those who fear you.

As far as the east is from the west,
so far have you removed our sins from us.

Ps. 103:8, 10–12

97

You are gracious and full of compassion, O Lord,
slow to anger and of great kindness.

You are loving to everyone
and your compassion is over all your works.

You are near to those who call upon you,
to all who call upon you faithfully.

You fulfill the desire of those who fear you;
you hear their cry and help them.

Ps. 145:8, 9, 18, 19

The following hymns or hymn stanzas are appropriate for use as responses to pardon:

	Hymnal	*Hymnbook*	*Worshipbook*
All Glory Be to God on High			283
Joyful, Joyful, We Adore Thee (st. 3)	5	21	446
Let Us with a Gladsome Mind	64	28	453
O for a Thousand Tongues to Sing	199	141	493
O Lord, You Are Our God and King			517
Praise God, from Whom All Blessings Flow	94*, 95*	544	224, 244, 266, 272
Praise, My Soul, the King of Heaven	14	31	551
Praise the Lord, His Glories Show (st. 3)	12	4	552
Praise the Lord! You Heavens, Adore Him (st. 2)	10	3	554
Sing Praise to God, Who Reigns Above		15	568
There's a Wideness in God's Mercy	93	110	601

*Section of *The Hymnal* entitled "Responses and Ancient Hymns and Canticles."

After the response to pardon, or at another place in the service, the people may exchange signs of God's peace.

98

When the peace follows the words of pardon:

Since God has forgiven us in Christ,
let us forgive one another.

The peace of our Lord Jesus Christ
be with you all.

Peace be with you.

John 20:19, 21, 26

99

When used at other times in the service:

Let the peace of Christ rule in your hearts.
To this peace we were called
as members of a single body.

The peace of Christ be with you.

Col. 3:15

Peace be with you.

John 20:19, 21, 26

100

When used at the end of the service:

Since Christ has opened his heart to us,
let us open our hearts to one another,
and God will be glorified.

The peace of Christ be with you.

Peace be with you.

John 20:19, 21, 26

101

Guide us, O God,
by your Word and Holy Spirit,
that in your light we may see light,
in your truth find freedom,
and in your will discover your peace;
through Jesus Christ our Lord.

Amen.

102

Prepare our hearts, O God,
to accept your Word.
Silence in us any voice but your own,
that, hearing, we may also obey your will;
through Jesus Christ our Lord.

Amen.

103

O God,
tell us what we need to hear,
and show us what we ought to do
to obey Jesus Christ.

Amen.

104

Lord, open our hearts and minds
by the power of your Holy Spirit,
that as the Scriptures are read
and your Word is proclaimed,
we may hear with joy what you say to us today.

Amen.

105
Gracious God,
give us humble, teachable, and obedient hearts,
that we may receive what you have revealed,
and do what you have commanded.
Since we do not live by bread alone,
but by every word that comes from your mouth,
make us hunger for this heavenly food,
that it may nourish us today
in the ways of eternal life;
through Jesus Christ, the bread of heaven.

Amen.

106
God our helper,
show us your ways and teach us your paths.
By your Holy Spirit,
open our minds
that we may be led in your truth
and taught your will.
Then may we praise you
by listening to your Word
and by obeying it;
through Jesus Christ our Lord.

Amen.

107
O Lord our God,
your Word is a lamp to our feet
and a light to our path.
Give us grace to receive your truth in faith and love,
that we may be obedient to your will
and live always for your glory,
through Jesus Christ our Savior.

Amen.

108
God, source of all light,
by your Word you give light to the soul.

Pour out upon us
the spirit of wisdom and understanding
that, being taught by you in Holy Scripture,
our hearts and minds may be opened to know the things
that pertain to life and holiness;
through Jesus Christ our Lord.

Amen.

109

Almighty God,
in you are hidden
all the treasures of wisdom and knowledge.
Open our eyes
that we may see the wonders of your Word;
and give us grace
that we may clearly understand
and freely choose the way of your wisdom;
through Jesus Christ our Lord.

Amen.

110

God of mercy,
you promised never to break your covenant with us.
Amid all the changing words of our generation,
may we hear your eternal Word that does not change.
Then may we respond to your gracious promises
with faithful and obedient lives;
through our Lord Jesus Christ.

Amen.

111

Blessed Lord,
who caused all holy Scriptures to be written for our learning:
Grant us so to hear them,
read, mark, learn, and inwardly digest them,
that we may embrace and ever hold fast
the blessed hope of everlasting life,
which you have given us in our Savior Jesus Christ.

Amen.

WORDS INTRODUCING THE READINGS FROM SCRIPTURE 112–115

112
A reading (lesson) from __________ .

113
Before the reading of the Gospel:

The holy Gospel of our Lord Jesus Christ according to __________.
Glory to you, O Lord.

114
The first (*or* Old Testament) lesson is __________ .
Hear the Word of God.

The second (*or* Epistle) lesson is __________ .
Hear the Word of God.

The Gospel lesson is __________ .
Hear the Word of God.

115
The first (*or* second *or* Gospel) lesson is __________ .
The Word of God.

WORDS CONCLUDING THE READINGS FROM SCRIPTURE 116–118

116
The Word of the Lord.
Thanks be to God.

117
This is the Word of the Lord.
Thanks be to God.

118
After the reading of the Gospel:

The Gospel of the Lord.
Praise to you, O Christ.

ASCRIPTIONS OF PRAISE 119–126

The following verses from Scripture ascribe glory to God. One may be used by the preacher as a prayer at the conclusion of the sermon.

119

Praise and glory and wisdom
and thanksgiving and honor
and power and strength
to our God for ever and ever. *Rev. 7:12*

Amen.

120

Now to the Ruler of all worlds,
undying, invisible, the only God,
be honor and glory for ever and ever! *I Tim. 1:17*

Amen.

121

Now to the One
who by the power at work within us
is able to do far more abundantly
than all we ask or think,
to God be glory in the church
and in Christ Jesus,
to all generations for ever and ever. *Eph. 3:20, 21*

Amen.

122

Worthy is the Lamb who was slain,
to receive power and wealth
and wisdom and might
and honor and glory and blessing! *Rev. 5:12*

Amen.

123
To Jesus Christ, who loves us
and has freed us from our sins by his blood
and made us a kingdom,
priests of his God and Father,
to him be glory and dominion
for ever and ever. *Rev. 1:5, 6*

Amen.

124
To the blessed and only sovereign,
the King of kings
and Lord of lords,
who alone has immortality
and dwells in unapproachable light,
be honor and eternal dominion. *I Tim. 6:15, 16*

Amen.

125
O the depth of the riches and wisdom and knowledge of God!
How unsearchable are God's judgments
and how inscrutable God's ways!
For from God
and through God
and to God are all things.
To God be glory forever. *Rom. 11:33, 36*

Amen.

126
To the God of all grace,
who calls you to share God's eternal glory
in union with Christ,
be the power forever! *I Peter 5:10, 11*

Amen.

INVITATIONS TO DISCIPLESHIP 127–134

The preacher may use any of the following Scripture verses in inviting persons to make or renew a personal commitment to Christ and his kingdom.

127
All who thirst, come to the waters.
All who have no money, come, buy and eat!
Come, buy wine and milk
without money and without price.
Why do you spend your money
for that which is not bread,
and your labor
for that which does not satisfy? *Isa. 55:1, 2*

128
Peter said,
"Repent and be baptized
in the name of Jesus Christ
for the forgiveness of your sins;
and you shall receive the gift of the Holy Spirit.
For the promise is to you and to your children
and to all that are far off,
everyone whom the Lord our God calls." *Acts 2:38, 39*

129
Jesus said to Simon and Andrew,
who were fishermen casting a net in the sea,
"Follow me
and I will make you fishers of people." *Mark 1:16, 17*

130
Come to me,
all you who labor and are heavily burdened,
and I will give you rest.
Take my yoke upon you,
and learn from me;
for I am gentle and lowly in heart,
and you will find rest for your souls.
For my yoke is easy,
and my burden is light. *Matt. 11:28–30*

131
Wash yourselves;
make yourselves clean,
remove the evil of your doings from before my eyes;
cease to do evil,
learn to do good;
seek justice, correct oppression;
defend the fatherless, plead for the widow.
Come now,
let us reason together, says the Lord:
though your sins are like scarlet,
I shall wash you as clean as snow;
though your sins are red like crimson,
they shall become like wool. *Isa. 1:16–18*

132
I appeal to you, brothers and sisters,
by the mercies of God,
to present your bodies as a living sacrifice,
holy and acceptable to God.
This is your spiritual worship.
Do not be conformed to this world
but be transformed by the renewal of your mind. *Rom. 12:1, 2*

133
When asked,
"What must I do to be saved?"
Paul and Silas answered,
"Believe in the Lord Jesus,
and you will be saved,
you and your family." *Acts 16:30, 31*

134
Jesus said,
"Behold, I stand at the door and knock;
if those who hear my voice open the door,
I will come in to them and eat with them,
and they with me." *Rev 3:20*

CREEDS OF THE CHURCH AND AFFIRMATIONS OF FAITH DRAWN FROM SCRIPTURE 135–143

When the Eucharist is celebrated, the Nicene Creed is traditionally used.

When Baptism is celebrated, the Apostles' Creed is included in relation to the baptism. No other creed or affirmation is needed.

On days when neither Sacrament is celebrated, the people join in a creed or statement of faith using any of the following. A Declaration of Faith *(1976) and* The Confession of 1967 *are useful resources from which statements of faith may be selected.*

135

THE NICENE CREED

We believe in one God,
the Father, the Almighty,
maker of heaven and earth,
of all that is, seen and unseen.

We believe in one Lord, Jesus Christ,
the only Son of God,
eternally begotten of the Father,
God from God, Light from Light,
true God from true God,
begotten, not made,
of one Being with the Father.
Through him all things were made.
For us and for our salvation
he came down from heaven:
by the power of the Holy Spirit
he became incarnate from the Virgin Mary, and was made human.
For our sake he was crucified under Pontius Pilate;
he suffered death and was buried.
On the third day he rose again
in accordance with the Scriptures;
he ascended into heaven
and is seated at the right hand of the Father.
He will come again in glory to judge the living and the dead,
and his kingdom will have no end.

We believe in the Holy Spirit, the Lord, the giver of life,
who proceeds from the Father and the Son.
With the Father and the Son he is worshiped and glorified.
He has spoken through the prophets.
We believe in one holy catholic and apostolic church.
We acknowledge one baptism for the forgiveness of sins.
We look for the resurrection of the dead,
and the life of the world to come. Amen.

136

THE APOSTLES' CREED

I believe in God, the Father almighty,
creator of heaven and earth.

I believe in Jesus Christ, his only Son, our Lord.
He was conceived by the power of the Holy Spirit
and born of the Virgin Mary.
He suffered under Pontius Pilate,
was crucified, died, and was buried.
He descended to the dead.
On the third day he rose again.
He ascended into heaven,
and is seated at the right hand of the Father.
He will come again to judge the living and the dead.

I believe in the Holy Spirit,
the holy catholic church,
the communion of saints,
the forgiveness of sins,
the resurrection of the body,
and the life everlasting. Amen.

137

Leader:
Who shall separate us from the love of Christ?
Shall tribulation or distress?
or persecution or famine?
or nakedness or peril or sword?

People:
No, in all these things
we are more than conquerors
through him who loved us.
For we are sure
that neither death nor life,
nor angels nor principalities,
nor things present nor things to come,
nor powers, nor height, nor depth,
nor anything else in all creation,
will be able to separate us
from the love of God
in Christ Jesus our Lord. Amen. *Rom. 8:35, 37–39*

138

We believe there is no condemnation
for those who are in Christ Jesus;
and we know that in everything God works for good
with those who love him,
who are called according to his purpose.
We are sure that neither death, nor life,
nor angels, nor principalities,
nor things present, nor things to come,
nor powers, nor height, nor depth,
nor anything else in all creation,
will be able to separate us
from the love of God
in Christ Jesus our Lord. Amen *Rom. 8:1, 28, 38, 39*

139

This is the good news
which we have received,
in which we stand,
and by which we are saved,
if we hold it fast:
that Christ died for our sins
according to the scriptures,
that he was buried,
that he was raised on the third day,

and that he appeared
first to the women,
then to Peter, and to the Twelve,
and then to many faithful witnesses.

We believe that Jesus is the Christ,
the Son of the living God.
Jesus Christ is the first and the last,
the beginning and the end;
he is our Lord and our God. Amen.

I Cor. 15:1–6
Mark 16:9 (16:1–9)
Matt. 16:16
Rev. 22:13
John 20:28

140

Jesus Christ is the image of the invisible God,
the firstborn of all creation;
In him all things in heaven and on earth were created,
things visible and invisible.

All were created through him;
all were created for him.
He is before all else that is.
In him everything continues in being.

It is he who is head of the body, the church!
he who is the beginning,
the firstborn of the dead,
so that he may be first in everything.

It pleased God
to make absolute fullness reside in him
and, by means of him,
to reconcile everything in his person,
both on earth and in the heavens,
making peace through the blood of his cross.

Col. 1:15–20

141

Christ Jesus,
though he was in the form of God,
did not count equality with God
a thing to be grasped,
but emptied himself,
taking the form of a servant,
being born in human likeness.

And being found in human form
he humbled himself
and became obedient unto death,
even death on a cross.

Therefore God has highly exalted him
and bestowed on him the name which is above every name,
that at the name of Jesus
every knee should bow,
in heaven and on earth and under the earth,
and every tongue confess to the glory of God:
Jesus Christ is Lord! Amen. *Phil. 2:5–11*

142

Jesus is Lord! *I Cor. 12:3; Rom. 10:9*

143

Jesus is the Christ,
the Son of the living God. *Matt. 16:16*

The congregation is invited to pray to God for the church universal, the world, those in authority, the community, persons in distressing circumstances, and those with special needs.

Many forms of intercession are available. It is desirable to use a variety of forms, giving ample opportunity for the people to participate actively. Following are six patterns to use in preparing for specific services. None is a complete prayer, since a wider range of concerns would need to be included. Those who lead worship may wish to use other suitable forms.

144

This form of intercession consists of a series of petitions. Each petition begins with a bidding to prayer, continues in silent prayer, and is concluded with a collect. The people respond with "Amen" or "Hear our prayer, O God." An example is included in The Worshipbook *(pages 31–33; prayers from pages 179–202 may be incorporated into such a prayer). Particular petitions will be selected or prepared for use in the service.*

Almighty God, in Jesus Christ you taught us to pray,
and promised that what we ask in his name will be given us.
Guide us by your Holy Spirit,
that our prayers for others may serve your will
and show your steadfast love;
through the same Jesus Christ our Lord.

Amen. (*Or,* **Hear our prayer, O God.)**

Let us pray for the world.

Silent prayer.

Creator God,
you made all things in your wisdom,
and in your love you save us.
We pray for the whole creation.
Order unruly powers, deal with injustice,
feed and satisfy those who thirst for justice,
so that your children may freely enjoy the earth you have made,
and cheerfully sing your praises;
through Jesus Christ our Lord.

Amen. (*Or*, Hear our prayer, O God.)

Let us pray for the church.

Silent prayer.

Gracious God,
you have called us to be the church of Jesus Christ.
Keep us one in faith and service,
breaking bread together, and telling the good news to the world,
that all may believe you are love,
turn to your ways,
and live to give you glory;
through Jesus Christ our Lord.

Amen. (*Or*, Hear our prayer, O God.)

Other petitions are added.

The prayer ends with commemorations of those who have died in the faith (150–154), and a concluding collect (155–166).

145

The litany is an effective form for intercession. In the following litany the series of petitions ends in identical words, thereby providing a cue for the congregation's response.

With all our heart and with all our mind,
let us pray to the Lord,
saying, "Lord, have mercy."

For the peace of the world,
for the welfare of the church of God,
and for the unity of all peoples,
let us pray to the Lord.

Lord, have mercy.

For our President,
for the leaders of the nations,
and for all in authority,
let us pray to the Lord.

Lord, have mercy.

For those who are poor and oppressed,
for those unemployed and destitute,
for prisoners and captives,
and for all who remember and care for them,
let us pray to the Lord.

Lord, have mercy.

Other petitions are included.

Here follow commemorations of those who have died in the faith:

For the faithful who have gone before us and are at rest,
let us give thanks to the Lord.

Alleluia.

Help, save, comfort, and defend us,
gracious Lord.

Silence.

Rejoicing in the fellowship of all saints,
let us commend ourselves,
one another,
and our whole life to Christ our Lord.

To you, O Lord.

A concluding collect ends the prayer (155–166).

146

In this bidding prayer, a series of concerns are named by members of the congregation, or by a leader. After each concern, the leader summarizes it with a call for prayer. Silence follows until the next concern is voiced.

Member (or leader):
I ask your prayers for God's people throughout the world;
for church leaders;
for this gathering;
and for all ministers and people.

Leader:
Pray for the church.

Silence.

Member (or leader):
I ask your prayers for peace;
for goodwill among nations;
and for the well-being of all people.

Leader:
Pray for justice and peace.

Silence.

Member (or leader):
I ask your prayers for all who seek deeper knowledge of God.

Leader:
Pray that they may find God
and be found by God.

Silence.

In a similar manner, other petitions are added.

Here follow commemorations of those who have died in the faith:

Member (or leader):
Praise God for those in every generation in whom God has been honored [especially __________, whom we remember today].

Leader:
Pray that we may have grace to glorify God in our own day.

Silence.

The prayer ends with a concluding collect (155–166).

147

Silent prayer is also included in this form of bidding prayer.

Let us pray for the church and for the world.

Grant, almighty God,
that all who confess your name may be united in your truth,
live together in your love,
and reveal your glory in the world.

Silence.

Lord, in your mercy,

hear our prayer.

Guide the people of this land, and of all the nations,
in the ways of justice and peace,
that we may honor one another and serve the common good.

Silence.

Lord, in your mercy,

hear our prayer.

Give us all a reverence for the earth as your creation,
that we may use its resources rightly,
in the service of others and to your honor and glory.

Silence.

Lord, in your mercy,

hear our prayer.

Bless all whose lives are closely linked with ours,
and grant that we may serve Christ in them,
and love one another as he loves us.

Silence.

Lord, in your mercy,

hear our prayer.

Other petitions are offered in the same manner.

The prayer ends with commemorations of those who have died in the faith (150–154), and a concluding collect (155–166).

148

Another form consists of a series of short prayers spoken by a leader, with the people responding to each with an "Amen," thereby affirming the prayers as their own.

Let us pray for our nation in a time of crisis.

O God, our help in ages past,
in your sight nations rise and fall, and pass through times of peril.
Be near to judge and save when our land is in trouble.
Grant our leaders your wisdom,
that they may search your will and see it clearly.
Where as a nation we have turned from your path,
reverse our ways and help us to repent.
Give your light and truth to guide;
through Jesus Christ, who is King of kings
and Lord of this world.

Amen.

Let us pray for those who are disabled.

God of compassion,
in Jesus Christ you cared for those who were blind or deaf,
crippled or slow to learn.
Though all of us need help,
give special care to those who are handicapped,
particularly those we name in silence. . . .
By our concern may they know the love you have for them,
and come to trust you;
through Jesus Christ who came to heal.

Amen.

Let us pray for those who do migrant work.

Eternal God,
your servant Jesus had no place to lay his head,
and no home to call his own.
We pray for men and women, for girls and boys,
who follow seasons and go where the work is,
who harvest crops or do part-time jobs.
Be with them in love,
so they may believe in you,
and be your pilgrim people, trusting in Jesus Christ the Lord.

Amen.

Let us pray for those who are unemployed.

God of compassion,
we remember those who suffer want and anxiety
because they have no work.
Guide the people of this land to use its wealth
so that all may find fulfilling employment
and receive just payment for their labor;
through Jesus Christ our Lord.

Amen.

Other petitions are offered in the same manner.

The prayer ends with commemorations of those who have died in the faith (150–154), and a concluding collect (155–166).

149

Another form of intercession consists of a number of petitions in connected paragraphs, with the people affirming them in an "Amen" at the conclusion.

Almighty and ever-living God,
by your apostle you taught us to pray
not only for ourselves but for others,
and to give thanks for all of life.

Inspire your whole church with the spirit of power, unity, and peace.
Grant that all who trust you may receive your Word,
and live together in love.

Lead all nations in the way of justice and goodwill.
Direct those who govern,
that they may rule fairly, maintain order,
uphold those in need, and defend oppressed people;
that this world may claim your rule and know true peace.

Give grace to all who proclaim the gospel
through Word and Sacrament and deeds of mercy,
that by their teaching and example
they may bring others into your fellowship.

Comfort and relieve, O Lord,
all who are in trouble . . .
sorrow . . . poverty . . . sickness . . . grief . . .
or any other need,
especially those known to us,
whom we name before you in silence. . . .
Heal them in body, mind, or circumstance,
working in them, by your grace,
wonders beyond all they may dream or hope;
through Jesus Christ our Savior.

Amen.

Commemorations of Those Who Have Died in the Faith

150

God of all times and places,
we praise you for all your servants
who, having been faithful to you on earth,
now live with you in heaven.
Keep us in fellowship with them,
until we meet with all your children
in the joy of your eternal kingdom;
through Jesus Christ our Lord.

Amen.

151

Almighty God, we remember before you
those who have lived among us
who have directed our steps in the way,
opened our eyes to the truth,
inspired our hearts by their witness,
and strengthened our wills by their devotion.
We rejoice in their lives dedicated to your service.
We honor them in their death,
and pray that we may be united with them
in the glory of Christ's resurrection.

Amen.

152

We give you thanks, O God,
for all who have fought the good fight
and finished their race
and kept the faith,
and for those dear to us
who are at rest with you. . . .

Grant us grace to follow them
as they followed Christ.
Bring us, with them, to those things
which no eye has seen, nor ear heard,
which you have prepared for those who love you.

To your name,
with the church on earth and the church in heaven,
we ascribe all honor and glory,
for ever and ever.

Amen.

153

O God,
before you the generations rise and pass away.
You are the strength of those who labor;
you are the rest of the blessed dead.
We rejoice in the company of your saints.
We remember all who have lived in faith,
all who have peacefully died,
and especially those dear to us who rest in you. . . .
Give us in time our portion with those who have trusted in you
and have striven to do your holy will.
To your name,
with the church on earth and the church in heaven,
we ascribe all honor and glory,
now and forever.

Amen.

154

Eternal God,
we remember with thanksgiving
those who have loved and served you in your church on earth,
who now rest from their labors
[especially those most dear to us,
whom we name in our hearts before you . . .].
Keep us in fellowship with all your saints,
and bring us at last
to the joy of your heavenly kingdom.

Amen.

Concluding Collects

155
Eternal God,
ruler of all things in heaven and earth,
accept the prayers of your people,
and strengthen us to do your will;
through Jesus Christ.

Amen.

156
Lord our God,
accept the fervent prayers of your people.
In your great mercy,
look with compassion on us
and all who turn to you for help,
for you are gracious, O lover of souls.
To you we give glory,
O blessed Trinity,
now and forever.

Amen.

157
Hear our prayers, God of grace,
and help us to enact them,
working for your peace and justice, mercy and purpose,
in all we do today;
through Jesus Christ the Lord.

Amen.

158
Hear our prayers, almighty God,
in the name of Jesus Christ,
who prays with us and for us.
To him be praise forever.

Amen.

159
Mighty God,
whose Word we trust,
whose Spirit prays in our prayers:
accept our requests
and further those which will bring your purpose for the earth;
through Jesus Christ, who rules over all things.

Amen.

160
Into your hands, O God,
we commend all for whom we pray,
trusting in your mercy;
through Jesus Christ our Lord.

Amen.

161
O God,
you made of one blood all races and nations of earth,
and you sent your Son Jesus Christ
to preach peace to those who are far off
and to those who are near.
Pour out your Spirit on the whole creation,
bring the nations of the world into your fellowship,
and hasten the coming of your kingdom;
through Jesus Christ our Lord.

Amen.

162
Lord Jesus Christ,
you stretched out your arms of love on the hard wood of the cross
that everyone might come within the reach of your saving embrace.
So clothe us in your Spirit
that we, reaching forth our hands in love,
may bring those who do not know you
to the knowledge and love of you;
for the honor of your name.

Amen.

163

Almighty God,
you have given us grace at this time with one accord
to make our common supplication to you;
and you have promised through your well-beloved Son
that when two or three are gathered together in his name
you will be in the midst of them.
Fulfill now, O Lord, our desires and petitions
as may be best for us;
granting us in this world knowledge of your truth,
and in the age to come life everlasting.

Amen.

164

O God,
the author of peace and lover of concord,
to know you is eternal life, to serve you is perfect freedom.
Guide us by your truth,
and order us in all our ways,
that we may always do what is right in your eyes,
through Jesus Christ our Lord.

Amen.

165

Eternal God,
you create us by your power and redeem us by your love.
Guide and strengthen us by your Spirit,
that we may give ourselves in love and service
to one another and to you, through Jesus Christ our Lord.

Amen.

166

God of mercy,
you have promised to hear what we ask in the name of Christ.
Accept and fulfill our petitions, we pray,
not as we ask in our ignorance,
nor as we deserve in our sinfulness,
but as you know and love us in Jesus Christ our Lord.

Amen.

SENTENCES INTRODUCING THE OFFERING 167–179

The offering is introduced with these words:

167
With gladness, let us present
the offerings of our life and labor to the Lord.

One of the verses given below, or other appropriate Scripture, follows.

168
Walk in love,
as Christ loved us
and gave himself up for us,
a fragrant offering and sacrifice to God. *Eph. 5:2*

169
The earth and all it contains belong to the Lord,
the world and those who live in it. *Ps. 24:1*

170
Do not lay up for yourselves treasures on earth,
where moth and rust consume
and where thieves break in and steal,
but lay up for yourselves treasures in heaven,
where neither moth nor rust consumes
and where thieves do not break in and steal.
For where your treasure is,
there will your heart be also. *Matt. 6:19–21*

171
Freely you have received,
freely give. *Matt. 10:8b*

172
Having gifts that differ according to the grace given us,
let us use them:
if service, in our serving;
whoever contributes, in liberality;
whoever does acts of mercy, with cheerfulness. *Rom. 12:6–8*

173

You know the grace of our Lord Jesus Christ:
though he was rich, yet for your sake he became poor,
so that by his poverty you might become rich. *II Cor. 8:9*

174

They who sow sparingly will also reap sparingly;
they who sow bountifully will also reap bountifully. *II Cor. 9:6*

175

Do as you have made up your mind,
not reluctantly or under compulsion,
for God loves a cheerful giver. *II Cor. 9:7*

176

Bear one another's burdens,
and so fulfill the law of Christ. *Gal. 6:2*

177

Do good and share what you have,
for such sacrifices are pleasing to God. *Heb. 13:16*

178

O Lord our God,
you are worthy to receive glory and honor and power;
because you have created all things,
and by your will
they were created and have their being. *Rev. 4:11*

179

Yours, O Lord, is the greatness,
the power, the glory, the victory, and the majesty.
For everything in heaven and on earth is yours.
Yours, O Lord, is the kingdom,
and you are exalted as head over all. *I Chron. 29:11*

Other Scripture verses that may be used to introduce the offering:

Deut. 15:11b
Deut. 16:17
Ps. 50:14
Ps. 96:8
Ps. 116:12, 14
Matt. 5:23, 24
Acts 20:35b
Rom. 12:1
I Cor. 4:2
I Cor. 9:10, 11
I John 3:17, 18

180

Friends, this is the joyful feast of the people of God!
They will come from east and west
and from north and south,
and sit at table in the kingdom of God. *Luke 13:29*

According to Luke,
when our risen Lord was at table with his disciples,
he took the bread, and blessed and broke it,
and gave it to them.
Then their eyes were opened
and they recognized him. *Luke 24:30, 31*

This is the Lord's table.
Our Savior invites those who trust him
to share the feast which he has prepared.

181

Hear the gracious words of our Savior Jesus Christ:

Come to me, all you who labor and are heavily burdened,
and I will give you rest.
Take my yoke upon you, and learn from me;
for I am gentle and lowly in heart,
and you will find rest for your souls. *Matt. 11:28, 29*

I am the bread of life.
Those who come to me shall not hunger,
and those who believe in me shall never thirst.
No one who comes to me will I cast out. *John 6:35, 37*

Happy are those who hunger and thirst
to do what is right, for they shall be filled. *Matt. 5:6*

182

Behold, I stand at the door and knock;
if those who hear my voice open the door,
I will come in to them and eat with them,
and they with me. *Rev. 3:20*

O taste and see that the Lord is good!
Happy are all who find refuge in God! *Ps. 34:8*

183

The Lord be with you.

And also with you.

Lift up your hearts.

We lift them to the Lord.

Let us give thanks to the Lord our God.

It is right to give our thanks and praise.

O holy God, Father almighty, Creator of heaven and earth,
with joy we give you thanks and praise.

Here follows the variation appropriate to the day or season.

ADVENT

In the words of the prophets
you comforted your people with the promise of the Redeemer,
and gave hope for the day when justice shall roll down like waters,
and righteousness like an ever-flowing stream.
Because you sent your Son to save us,
the day of our deliverance has dawned.
We rejoice that in Christ you will make all things new
when he comes again in power and great glory
to claim his kingdom and hand it over to you.

The prayer continues on page 96.

NATIVITY OF JESUS CHRIST / CHRISTMAS

In sending us your Son, Jesus, to be born of Mary,
your Word became flesh
and we have seen a new and radiant vision of your glory.
His name is above every name.
He is light in our darkness,
the Prince of peace and Savior of all,
for in him we are delivered from sin
and given the power to become your children.

The prayer continues on page 96.

EPIPHANY

In sending Christ the Light of the world,
you revealed your glory to the nations.
You sent a star to guide seekers of wisdom to Bethlehem,
that they might worship Christ;
your signs and witnesses in every age
lead people from every place to worship him.
We praise you that through him we are saved
and baptized into your service.

The prayer continues on page 96.

BAPTISM OF THE LORD

In being baptized by John in Jordan's waters,
Jesus identified himself with sinners
and your voice proclaimed him as your Son.
Like a dove, your Spirit descended on him,
anointing him as the Christ,
sent to preach good news to the poor
and proclaim release to the captives;
to recover sight for the blind
and set free the oppressed;
to announce that the time had come
when you would save your people.
We praise you that in our baptism we are joined to Christ
and, with all the baptized, are called to share his ministry.

The prayer continues on page 96.

TRANSFIGURATION OF THE LORD

On the holy mountain,
the divine glory of the incarnate Word was revealed.
From the heavens your voice proclaimed your beloved Son,
who is the fulfillment of the law and the prophets.
We rejoice in the divine majesty of Christ,
whose glory shone forth even when confronted with the cross.

The prayer continues on page 96.

LENT

We need not hide ourselves from you,
before whose justice none can stand.
Your mercy was proclaimed by the apostles and the prophets,
and shown forth to us in Jesus Christ.
You give your law to guide us,
and you promise new life for all,
that we may live to serve you among our neighbors
in all we do and say.

The prayer continues on page 96.

PASSION SUNDAY / PALM SUNDAY

Your Son Jesus fulfilled the prophets' words
and entered the city of Jerusalem,
where he was lifted high upon the cross,
that the whole world might be drawn to him.
By his suffering and death
he became the source of eternal life.
The tree of defeat became the tree of victory,
for where life was lost,
there life has been restored.

The prayer continues on page 96.

MAUNDY THURSDAY

Your beloved Son came as a servant
to wash away our pride
and feed us with the bread of life.
We thank you
for inviting us to feast with him who died for us,
and who calls us to serve each other in love.

The prayer continues on page 96.

GOOD FRIDAY

By your Son Jesus,
who was condemned, forsaken, and hanged on a cross,
we are forgiven.

We are thankful that he obeyed you and died
to show us that we are not forsaken or condemned,
but will live in paradise with him.

The prayer continues on page 96.

RESURRECTION OF THE LORD / EASTER

By your own power you raised Christ Jesus from death to life.
Through his victory over the grave
we are set free from the bonds of sin and the fear of death
to share the glorious freedom of the children of God.
In his rising to life
you promise eternal life to all who believe in him.
We praise you that as we break bread in faith,
we shall know the risen Christ among us.

The prayer continues on page 96.

ASCENSION OF THE LORD

You raised up Christ to rule over all creation,
giving him the name which is above all other names,
that at the name of Jesus every knee shall bow.
We praise you that, lifted in power,
he lives and reigns forever in your glory
and so fulfills his promise to be with us always
to the end of time.

The prayer continues on page 96.

PENTECOST SUNDAY

In fulfillment of Christ's promise,
you poured out the Holy Spirit upon the chosen disciples
and filled the church with power.
We thank you for sending your Spirit to us today
to kindle faith and teach the truth of your Son Jesus,
working in the church to make us faithful disciples,
and empowering us to proclaim the living Christ to every nation.

The prayer continues on page 96.

TRINITY SUNDAY

You revealed your glory
as the glory also of your Son and of the Holy Spirit,
three Persons, equal in majesty, undivided in splendor,
yet one Lord, one God,
to be worshiped and adored in your eternal glory.
We praise you,
Father, Son, and Holy Spirit,
great Trinity of power and love,
our God, for ever and ever.

The prayer continues on page 96.

ALL SAINTS' DAY (or Sunday following)

We praise you today
for saints and martyrs, faithful people in every age,
who have followed your Son
and witnessed to his resurrection,
that, strengthened by their witness
and supported by their fellowship,
we may run with perseverance the race that lies before us,
and with them receive the unfading crown of glory.

The prayer continues on page 96.

CHRIST THE KING

You exalted the risen Christ to rule over all creation,
that he might present to you an eternal and universal kingdom:
a kingdom of truth and life,
a kingdom of holiness and grace,
a kingdom of justice, love, and peace.

The prayer continues on page 96.

GENERAL I

You commanded light to shine out of darkness,
divided the sea and dry land,
created the vast universe and called it good.
You made us in your image to live with one another in love.
You gave us the breath of life
and freedom to choose your way.
You set forth your purpose in commandments through Moses,
and called for justice in the cry of prophets.
Through long generations
you have been patient and kind to all your children.

The prayer continues on page 96.

GENERAL II

You commanded light to shine out of darkness,
stretched out the heavens,
and laid the foundations of the earth.
You made all things through your Word.
We thank you for creating us in your image
and for keeping us in your steadfast love.
We praise you for calling us to be your people,
for revealing your purpose in the law and the prophets,
and for dealing patiently with our pride and disobedience.

The prayer continues on page 96.

GENERAL III (Unity or Worldwide Church;
World Communion Sunday)

You formed the universe in your wisdom,
and created all things by your power.
You set us in families on the earth
to live with you in faith.
We praise you for good gifts of bread and wine,
and for the table you spread in the world
as a sign of your love for all people in Christ.

The prayer continues on page 96.

BAPTISM

Through the waters of baptism we are buried with Christ
so that we may rise with him to new life.
We praise you for receiving us as your sons and daughters
for making us citizens of your kingdom,
and for giving us the Holy Spirit to guide us into all truth.

The prayer continues on page 96.

COMMISSIONING (CONFIRMATION)

By the Holy Spirit you lead us into all truth,
and give us power to proclaim your gospel to the nations
and to serve you as your priestly people.

The prayer continues on page 96.

ORDINATION

You sent your Son Jesus Christ,
who came not to be served but to serve,
and to give his life a ransom for many.
We praise you that he calls his faithful servants
to lead your holy people in love;

For the ordination of a minister of Word and Sacrament, add:

[to proclaim your Word
and to celebrate the Sacraments of the new covenant.]

The prayer continues on page 96.

CHRISTIAN MARRIAGE I

You formed us in your image;
male and female you created us.
You gave us the covenant of marriage
that we might know and be known.
Your love has been unfailing to your people in every age.
From bondage to freedom you led the house of Israel.
From exile and unfaithfulness you summoned her home.

Through Christ's death your church was sanctified,
that she might be holy and blameless,
like a bride pure and resplendent.
Happy are those who are invited to the wedding banquet of the Lamb.

The prayer continues on page 96.

CHRISTIAN MARRIAGE II

You created us male and female
and gave us the communion of one flesh.
You blessed Abraham and Sarah with offspring as numerous as stars.
By your providence you revealed Rebecca to Isaac.
By your grace Jacob labored for Rachel.
Through Christ you gladdened the wedding at Cana,
changing water into wine.
At this feast of joy you again manifest your glory.

The prayer continues on page 96.

CHRISTIAN BURIAL (or Memorial Service)

You sent to us your Son Jesus Christ,
who died and rose again to save us.
By his death on the cross
you revealed that your love has no limit.
By raising him from the grave
you comfort us with the blessed hope of eternal life.
By his victory
you assure us that neither death nor life,
nor things present nor things to come,
can separate us from your love in Christ Jesus our Lord.

The prayer continues on page 96.

The great prayer of thanksgiving continues:

How wonderful are your ways, almighty God.
How marvelous is your name, O Holy One.
You alone are God.
Therefore with apostles and prophets,
and that great cloud of witnesses
who live for you beyond all time and space,
we lift our hearts in joyful praise:

Holy, holy, holy Lord, God of power and might,
heaven and earth are full of your glory.
Hosanna in the highest.

Blessed is he who comes in the name of the Lord.
Hosanna in the highest.

We praise you, most holy God,
for sending your only Son Jesus to live among us,
full of grace and truth.
He made you known to all who received him.
Sharing our joy and sorrow,
he healed the sick and was a friend of sinners.

Obeying you,
he took up his cross and died that we might live.
We praise you that he overcame death
and is risen to rule the world.
He is still the friend of sinners.
We trust him to overcome every power that can hurt or divide us,
and believe that when he comes in glory
we will celebrate victory with him.

The words of institution may be said here or in relation to the breaking of the bread.

[We thank you that on the night before he died,
Jesus took bread, gave thanks to you, broke the bread,
and gave it to his disciples, saying,
"Take, eat.
This is my body, given for you.
Do this for the remembrance of me."

In the same way he took the cup, saying,
"This cup is the new covenant sealed in my blood,
shed for you for the forgiveness of sins.
Do this for the remembrance of me."]

Therefore, in remembrance of your mighty acts in Jesus Christ,
we take this bread and this cup
and give you praise and thanksgiving.

Let us proclaim the mystery of faith:

Christ has died,
Christ is risen,
Christ will come again.

Gracious God,
pour out your Holy Spirit upon us,
that this bread and this cup
may be for us the body and blood of our Lord,
and that we, and all who share this feast,
may be one with Christ and he with us.
Fill us with eternal life,
that with joy we may be his faithful people
until we feast with him in glory.

Through Christ, with Christ, in Christ,
in the unity of the Holy Spirit,
all glory and honor are yours, almighty Father,
for ever and ever.

Amen.

Our Father . . .

184

The bracketed portion of this prayer may be replaced, according to the time of the church year, by a seasonal variation from Great Prayer of Thanksgiving A (pages 88–95) or C (pages 102–103).

The Lord be with you.

And also with you.

Lift up your hearts.

We lift them to the Lord.

Let us give thanks to the Lord our God.

It is right to give our thanks and praise.

Eternal and ever-living God,
it is right to bless you,
to give thanks to you,
and to worship you in every place where your glory abides;

[for you laid the foundation of the earth,
and the heavens are the work of your hands.
They shall perish, but you shall endure,
for you are always the same
and your years will never end.

You made us in your image
and called us to be your people.
But we turned from you,
and sin established its reign by way of death.
Still you loved us and sought us.
In Christ your grace defeated death
and opened the way to eternal life.]

Therefore we praise you,
joining our voice with choirs of angels,
and with all the faithful of every time and place,
who forever sing to the glory of your name:

Holy, holy, holy Lord, God of power and might,
heaven and earth are full of your glory.
Hosanna in the highest.

Blessed is he who comes in the name of the Lord.
Hosanna in the highest.

Holy God,
in your mercy you sent the One in whom your fullness dwells,
your only-begotten,
to be for us the way, the truth, and the life.
In Jesus, born of Mary, your Word became flesh
and dwelt among us, full of grace and truth.

We glorify you for your great power and mercy at work in Christ.
By his suffering and death on the cross,
our sins are forgiven.
In rising from the grave,
he won for us victory over death.
We praise you that Christ our life now reigns with you in glory,
praying for us,
until all things are made perfect in Christ.

The words of institution may be said here or in relation to the breaking of the bread.

[We give you thanks
that when he was about to surrender himself to suffering,
Jesus took bread.
After giving thanks to you, he broke the bread
and gave it to his disciples, saying,
"Take, eat.
This is my body, given for you.
Do this in remembrance of me."

In the same way he took the cup, saying,
"This cup is the new covenant sealed in my blood,
shed for you for the forgiveness of sins.
Do this in remembrance of me."]

Let us proclaim the mystery of faith:

Christ has died,
Christ is risen,
Christ will come again.

Remembering these your mighty acts in Jesus Christ,
we take this bread and wine
and joyfully celebrate this holy Sacrament.
With praise and thanksgiving
we offer ourselves to you to be a living sacrifice,
dedicated to your service.

Gracious God,
pour out your Holy Spirit on us,
and on these your gifts of bread and wine,
that in eating this bread and drinking this cup,
we may know the presence of Christ
and be made one with him,
and one with all who come to this table.

In union with your church in heaven and on earth,
we pray that you will fulfill your eternal purpose
in us and in all the world.

Intercessions may be included such as the following:

[Remember your church.
Unite it in the truth of your Word
and empower it in ministry to the world.

Remember the world of nations.
By your Spirit renew the face of the earth;
let peace and justice prevail.

Remember our family and friends.
Bless them and watch over them;
be gracious to them and give them peace.

Remember the sick and the suffering,
the aged and the dying.
Encourage them and give them hope.

Rejoicing in the communion of saints,
we remember with thanksgiving
all your faithful servants, and those dear to us,
whom you have called from this life. . . .
We are grateful that for them death is no more,
nor is there sorrow, crying, or pain,
for the former things have passed away.]

Keep us in communion with all the faithful
from every time and place,
until we rejoice together in your eternal realm.

Through Christ, with Christ, in Christ,
in the unity of the Holy Spirit,
all glory and honor are yours, almighty God,
now and forever.

Amen.

Our Father . . .

GREAT PRAYER OF THANKSGIVING C

185

The Lord be with you.

And also with you.

Lift up your hearts.

We lift them to the Lord.

Let us give thanks to the Lord our God.

It is right to give our thanks and praise.

It is indeed right,
our duty and delight,
that we should at all times and in all places
give thanks to you, O holy Lord,
Father almighty, eternal God.

You created the heavens and the earth
and all that is in them;
you made us in your own image;
and in countless ways you show us your mercy.

A seasonal variation may be added here.

ADVENT

We praise you
that in the coming of your Son Jesus Christ,
your promises given by the prophets were fulfilled
and the day of our deliverance has dawned.
As we look for the triumph of his kingdom,
we exult with holy joy.

NATIVITY OF JESUS CHRIST / CHRISTMAS

We praise you,
because you sent Jesus Christ, your only Son,
to be born for us of Mary,
that we might be delivered from sin,
and receive power to become your children.

EPIPHANY

We praise you,
for in Jesus Christ,
the mystery of the Word made flesh,
you sent a light to shine upon the world,
that he might bring us out of darkness
into your marvelous light.

LENT

We praise you for Jesus Christ,
who was tempted in every way we are, yet without sin,
and who, having overcome temptation,
is able to help us in our times of trial,
and to give us strength to take up the cross
and follow him.

RESURRECTION OF THE LORD / EASTER

Above all we praise you
for the glorious resurrection of your Son,
Jesus Christ our Lord,
He is the true Passover Lamb
who takes away the sin of the world.
By his death he destroyed death,
and by his rising brought us eternal life.

PENTECOST SUNDAY

We praise you
that according to the promise of Jesus Christ
the Holy Spirit came upon the whole church,
that the everlasting gospel
should be preached among all people
to bring them out of darkness
into the clear light of your truth.

The great prayer of thanksgiving continues:

Therefore, with choirs of angels,
and the whole company of heaven,
we worship and adore your glorious name,
joining our voices in their unending praise:

Holy, holy, holy Lord, God of power and might,
heaven and earth are full of your glory.
Hosanna in the highest.

Blessed is he who comes in the name of the Lord.
Hosanna in the highest.

All glory and blessing are yours, O holy Father,
for in your great mercy
you gave your only Son Jesus Christ.
He took our human nature,
and suffered death on the cross for our redemption.
There he made a perfect sacrifice
for the sins of the whole world.

We praise you that before he suffered and died,
our Savior gave us this holy Sacrament
and commanded us to continue it
as a lasting memorial of his death and sacrifice
until he comes again.

The words of institution may be said here or in relation to the breaking of the bread.

[For on the night of his betrayal,
the Lord Jesus took bread.
After giving thanks to you,
he broke the bread
and gave it to his disciples, saying,
"Take, eat;
this is my body which is broken for you.
Do this in remembrance of me."

In the same way he took the cup, saying,
"This cup is the new covenant sealed in my blood,
shed for you for the forgiveness of sins.
Do this in remembrance of me."]

Therefore,
remembering his incarnation and holy life,
his death and glorious resurrection,
his ascension and continual intercession for us,
and awaiting his coming again in power and great glory,
we claim his eternal sacrifice
and celebrate with these your holy gifts
the memorial your Son commanded us to make.

Let us proclaim the mystery of faith:

Christ has died,
Christ is risen,
Christ will come again.

Merciful God,
by your Holy Spirit bless and make holy
both us and these your gifts of bread and wine,
that the bread we break
may be the communion of the body of Christ,
and the cup we bless
may be the communion of the blood of Christ.

Here we offer ourselves to be a living sacrifice,
holy and acceptable to you.
In your mercy,
accept our sacrifice of praise and thanksgiving.
In communion with all the faithful in heaven and on earth,
we ask you to fulfill, in us and in all creation,
the purpose of your redeeming love.

Through Christ, with Christ, in Christ,
in the unity of the Holy Spirit,
all glory and honor are yours, almighty Father,
now and forever.

Amen.

Our Father . . .

186

The Lord be with you.

And also with you.

Lift up your hearts.

We lift them to the Lord.

Let us give thanks to the Lord our God.

It is right to give our thanks and praise.

We give you thanks, O God,
through your beloved Servant, Jesus Christ,
whom you have sent in these last times
as Savior and Redeemer,
and Messenger of your will.

He is your Word,
inseparable from you,
through whom you made all things
and in whom you take delight.
He is your Word,
sent from heaven into the Virgin's womb,
where he was conceived,
and took on our nature and our lot,
was revealed as your Son
and was born of the Virgin by the power of the Holy Spirit.

It is he who fulfilled all your will
and won for you a holy people
when he stretched out his hands in suffering
to release from suffering those who place their trust in you.

It is he who freely accepted the death to which he was handed over,
in order to destroy death
and to shatter the chains of the evil one;
to trample underfoot the powers of hell
and to lead the righteous into light;
to fix the boundaries of death
and to make manifest the resurrection.

And so he took bread, gave thanks to you, and said:
"Take, eat;
this is my body, broken for you."
In the same way he took the cup, saying:
"This is my blood, shed for you.
When you do this, do it for the remembrance of me."

Remembering therefore his death and resurrection,
we set before you this bread and cup,
giving you thanks that you have counted us worthy
to stand in your presence and serve you as your priestly people.

We ask you to send your Holy Spirit upon the offering of the holy church,
gathering into one all who share these holy mysteries,
filling us with the Holy Spirit
and confirming our faith in the truth,
that together we may praise you and give you glory,
through your Servant, Jesus Christ.

Through him all glory and honor are yours, almighty Father,
with the Holy Spirit
in the holy church
now and forever.

Amen.

Our Father . . .

Since the words of institution are included in this prayer, they are not said in relation to the breaking of the bread.

187

The Lord be with you.

And also with you.

Lift up your hearts.

We lift them to the Lord.

Let us give thanks to the Lord our God.

It is right to give our thanks and praise.

It is truly right to glorify you, Father,
and to give you thanks,
for you alone are God, living and true,
dwelling in light inaccessible from before time and forever.

Fountain of all life and source of all goodness,
you made all things and fill them with your blessing;
you created them to rejoice in the splendor of your radiance.

Countless throngs of angels stand before you
to serve you night and day,
and, beholding the glory of your presence,
they offer you unceasing praise.
Joining with them,
and giving voice to every creature under heaven,
we acclaim you, and glorify your name, as we sing (say),

**Holy, holy, holy Lord, God of power and might,
heaven and earth are full of your glory.
Hosanna in the highest.**

**Blessed is he who comes in the name of the Lord.
Hosanna in the highest.**

We acclaim you, holy Lord, glorious in power;
your mighty works reveal your wisdom and love.
You formed us in your own image,
giving the whole world into our care,
so that, in obedience to you, our Creator,
we might rule and serve all your creatures.
When our disobedience took us far from you,
you did not abandon us to the power of death.

In your mercy you came to our help,
so that in seeking you we might find you.
Again and again you called us into covenant with you,
as the prophets taught us to hope for salvation.

Father, you loved the world so much
that in the fullness of time you sent your only Son to be our Savior.
Incarnate by the Holy Spirit, born of the Virgin Mary,
he lived as one of us, yet without sin.
To the poor he proclaimed the good news of salvation;
to prisoners, freedom; to the sorrowful, joy.
To fulfill your purpose he gave himself up to death;
and, rising from the grave,
destroyed death and made the whole creation new.
And that we might live no longer for ourselves
but for him who died and rose for us,
he sent the Holy Spirit,
his own first gift for those who believe,
to complete his work in the world,
and to bring to fulfillment the sanctification of all.

When the hour had come for him to be glorified
by you, his heavenly Father,
having loved his own who were in the world,
he loved them to the end:
at supper with them he took bread,
and gave thanks,
broke it, and gave it to his disciples, saying: "Take, eat.
This is my body, which is given for you.
Do this for the remembrance of me."

After supper he took the cup,
gave thanks to you, and gave it for all to drink, saying,
"This cup is the new covenant sealed in my blood,
shed for you and for all for the forgiveness of sins.
Do this for the remembrance of me."

Father, we now celebrate this memorial of our redemption.
Recalling Christ's death and his descent among the dead,
proclaiming his resurrection and ascension to your right hand,
awaiting his coming in glory;
and offering to you, from the gifts you have given us,
this bread and this cup,
we praise you and we bless you.

We praise you, we bless you,
we give thanks to you,
and we pray to you, Lord our God.

Lord, we pray that in your goodness and mercy
your Holy Spirit may descend upon us, and upon these gifts,
sanctifying them and showing them to be
holy gifts for your holy people,
the bread of life and the cup of salvation,
the body and blood of your Son Jesus Christ.

Grant that all who share this bread and cup
may become one body and one spirit,
a living sacrifice in Christ,
to the praise of your name.

Remember, Lord, your one holy catholic and apostolic church,
redeemed by the blood of your Christ.
Reveal its unity, guard its faith, and preserve it in peace.

[Remember (NN. and) all who minister in your church.]
[Remember all your people,
and those who seek your truth.]
[Remember __________ .]
[Remember all who have died in the peace of Christ,
and those whose faith is known to you alone;
bring them into the place of eternal joy and light.]

And grant that we may find our inheritance with

[the blessed Virgin Mary, with patriarchs, prophets, apostles,
and martyrs, and]

all the saints who have found favor with you in ages past.
We praise you in union with them and give you glory
through your Son Jesus Christ our Lord.

Through Christ, and with Christ, and in Christ,
all honor and glory are yours, almighty God and Father,
in the unity of the Holy Spirit,
for ever and ever.

Amen.

Our Father . . .

Since the words of institution are included in this prayer, they are not said in relation to the breaking of the bread.

188

The preface following the dialogue may be varied. Local congregations and eucharistic communities are encouraged to make their own decisions about its content and style, focusing on general themes stressing the creation, the season or day in the church year, or a local occasion. Proper prefaces for seasons of the church year are provided below.

The Lord be with you.

And also with you.

Lift up your hearts.

We lift them to the Lord.

Let us give thanks to the Lord our God.

It is right to give our thanks and praise.

Here follows the variation appropriate to the day or season.

ADVENT

It is right and good to give you thanks, almighty God.
You sent your servant John the Baptist to preach repentance
and to prepare the way of our Lord Jesus Christ.
Therefore, in all times and places
your people proclaim your glory in unending praise:

The prayer continues on page 113.

CHRISTMAS

It is right and good to give you thanks, almighty God.
You gave us the gift of your Son Jesus,
who is the light in this dark world
and our only Savior.
Therefore, in all times and places
your people proclaim your glory in unending praise:

The prayer continues on page 113.

EPIPHANY

It is right and good to give you thanks, almighty God.
You have given us the Word made flesh,
and through our baptism
we are blessed to share in the healing and reconciling love of Christ.
Therefore, in all times and places
your people proclaim your glory in unending praise:

The prayer continues on page 113.

LENT

It is right and good to give you thanks, almighty God.
You call us to cleanse our hearts
and prepare with joy for the victory of the Lamb who is slain.
Therefore, in all times and places
your people proclaim your glory in unending praise:

The prayer continues on page 113.

EASTER

It is right and good to give you thanks, almighty God.
You have brought forth our Lord Jesus from the grave.
By his death he has destroyed death,
and by his rising to life again
he has won for us everlasting life.
Therefore, in all times and places
your people proclaim your glory in unending praise:

The prayer continues on page 113.

PENTECOST

It is right and good to give you thanks, almighty God.
You poured out the Holy Spirit upon the disciples
teaching them the truth of your Son Jesus,
empowering your church for its service,
and uniting us as your holy people.
Therefore, in all times and places
your people proclaim your glory in unending praise:

The prayer continues on page 113.

GENERAL

It is right and good to give you thanks, almighty God,
for you are the source of light and life.
You made us in your image
and called us to new life in Jesus Christ.
In all times and places
your people proclaim your glory in unending praise:

The great prayer of thanksgiving continues:

Holy, holy, holy Lord, God of power and might,
heaven and earth are full of your glory.
Hosanna in the highest.

Blessed is he who comes in the name of the Lord.
Hosanna in the highest.

We remember with joy the grace by which you created all things
and made us in your own image.
We rejoice that you called a people in covenant
to be a light to the nations.
Yet we rebelled against your will.
In spite of prophets and pastors sent forth to us,
we continued to break your covenant.
In the fullness of time,
you sent your only Son to save us.
Incarnate by the Holy Spirit,
born of your favored one, Mary,
sharing our life, he reconciled us to your love.
At the Jordan your Spirit descended upon him,
anointing him to preach the good news of your reign.
He healed the sick and fed the hungry,
manifesting the power of your compassion.
He sought out the lost and broke bread with sinners,
witnessing the fullness of your grace.
We beheld his glory.

On the night before he died for us, Jesus took bread;
giving thanks to you, he broke the bread
and offered it to his disciples, saying:
"Take this and eat;
this is my body which is given for you;
do this in remembrance of me."

Taking a cup, again he gave thanks to you,
shared the cup with his disciples and said:
"This is the cup of the new covenant in my blood.
Drink from this, all of you.
This is poured out for you and for all,
for the forgiveness of sins."

After the meal our Lord was arrested,
abandoned by his followers, and beaten.
He stood trial and was put to death on a cross.
Having emptied himself in the form of a servant,
and being obedient even to death,
he was raised from the dead
and exalted as Lord of heaven and earth.

Through him you bestow the gift of your Spirit,
uniting your church,
empowering its mission,
and leading us into the new creation you have promised.
Gracious God,
we celebrate with joy the redemption won for us in Jesus Christ.
Grant that in praise and thanksgiving
we may be a living sacrifice,
holy and acceptable in your sight,
that our lives may proclaim the mystery of faith:

Christ has died,
Christ is risen,
Christ will come again.

Loving God,
pour out your Holy Spirit upon us and upon these gifts,
that they may be for us the body and blood of our Savior Jesus Christ.
Grant that we may be for the world the body of Christ,
redeemed through his blood,
serving and reconciling all people to you.

Remember your church, scattered upon the face of the earth;
gather it in unity and preserve it in truth.
Remember the saints who have gone before us
[especially __________ and __________ *(special names may be mentioned here)*].

In communion with them and with all creation,
we worship and glorify you always:

Through your Son Jesus Christ,
with the Holy Spirit in your holy church,
all glory and honor is yours, almighty God,
now and forever.

Amen.

Our Father . . .

Since the words of institution are included in this prayer, they are not said in relation to the breaking of the bread.

189

The Lord be with you.

And also with you.

Lift up your hearts.

We lift them to the Lord.

Let us give thanks to the Lord our God.

It is right to give our thanks and praise.

Almighty Father, creator and sustainer of life,
your majesty and power, your continued blessings,
and your great goodness fill us with wonder.
We are unworthy of the pardon you have in mercy given.
We can bring only our thanks,
putting our trust in your Son, who alone saves us from evil.

Therefore, in joy,
with prophets, apostles, martyrs, and saints of every time and place,
we join in giving you praise:

**Holy, holy, holy Lord, God of power and might,
heaven and earth are full of your glory.
Hosanna in the highest.**

**Blessed is he who comes in the name of the Lord.
Hosanna in the highest.**

God of glory,
in thanks we remember how Jesus broke bread and gave the cup
to make us partakers of his body and blood,
so that he might live in us and we in him.

God of mercy,
in thanks we remember how Jesus invites us to his table,
imprinting on our hearts his sacrifice on the cross.
In gratitude we bow before the Righteous One,
declaring his resurrection and glory,
and knowing that his prayers alone
make us worthy to partake of his spiritual meal.

Believing Christ's promise of eternal life,
we live in him and declare:

Christ has died,
Christ is risen,
Christ will come again.

Almighty God,
pour out your Holy Spirit upon us,
that as we receive bread and wine
we may be assured
that Christ's promise in these signs will be fulfilled.

Eternal Father,
lift our hearts and minds on high
where, with Christ your only Son,
and with the Holy Spirit,
all glory is yours,
now and forevermore.

Amen.

Our Father . . .

When this prayer is used, the words of institution are said in relation to the breaking of the bread.

190

This prayer is provided for use when serving Communion in the home or hospital, or other informal situations. The dialogue and memorial acclamation may be added.

Holy God, we praise you.
Let the heavens be joyful,
and the earth be glad.

We bless you for creating the whole world,
for your promises to your people Israel,
and for the life we know in Jesus Christ your Son.

Born of Mary, he shares our life.
Eating with sinners, he welcomes us.
Leading his followers, he guides us.
Dying on the cross, he rescues us.
Risen from the dead, he gives new life.

With thanksgiving we take this bread and this cup
and proclaim his death and resurrection.
Receive our sacrifice of praise.

Send to us your Holy Spirit
that this meal may be holy
and your people may become one.
Unite us in faith, inspire us to love,
encourage us with hope,
that we may receive Christ as he comes to us in this holy banquet.

We praise you, almighty Father,
through Christ your Son,
in the Holy Spirit.

Amen.

Our Father . . .

When this prayer is used, the words of institution are said in relation to the breaking of the bread.

"HOLY, HOLY, HOLY LORD" 191–192

Either of the following forms of the "Holy, holy, holy Lord" may be used.

191

Holy, holy, holy Lord, God of power and might,
heaven and earth are full of your glory.
Hosanna in the highest.

Blessed is he who comes in the name of the Lord.
Hosanna in the highest.

192

Holy, holy, holy Lord, God of power and might,
heaven and earth are full of your glory.
Hosanna in the highest.

MEMORIAL ACCLAMATIONS 193–196

One of the following acclamations may be used whenever a memorial acclamation occurs in a great prayer of thanksgiving.

193

Christ has died,
Christ is risen,
Christ will come again.

194

We remember his death,
we proclaim his resurrection,
we await his coming in glory.

195

When we eat this bread and drink this cup,
we proclaim your death, Lord Jesus,
until you come in glory.

196

Dying you destroyed our death,
rising you restored our life.
Lord Jesus, come in glory.

DOXOLOGICAL STANZAS

The last stanza of each of these hymns is a trinitarian praise appropriate for singing at the end of the great prayer of thanksgiving, or as sung praise at the conclusion of the Communion service. Those with Alleluias (A) are particularly appropriate for use during the Easter season, but not during Lent.

	Hymnal	*Hymnbook*	*Worshipbook*
All Creatures of Our God and King (A)		100	282
All Praise to Thee, Our God, This Night	42	63	292
Angel Voices, Ever Singing	455	30	
Awake, My Soul, and with the Sun		50	
Book of Books, Our People's Strength		248	
Christ Is Made the Sure Foundation	336	433	325
Come, Holy Ghost, Our Souls Inspire		237	335
Come, O Thou God of Grace	483		339
Come, Thou Almighty King	52	244	343
Come, You Faithful, Raise the Strain (A)			344
Creator of the Stars of Night			348
Father, We Praise You	24	43	365
For All the Saints (A)		425	369
Glory Be to God the Father (stanza 1)	60		
Glory Be to the Father	93*	545, 546	214, 236, 254, 272
Holy God, We Praise Your Name			420
Holy, Holy, Holy!	57	11	421
Jesus Christ Is Risen Today (A)	163	204	440
Now Thank We All Our God	459	9	481
Of the Father's Love Begotten	85*	7	534
Praise God, from Whom All Blessings Flow	94*, 95*	544	224, 244, 266, 272
Thou, Whose Almighty Word	392		
Ye Watchers and Ye Holy Ones (A)		34	

Section of The Hymnal *entitled "Responses and Ancient Hymns and Canticles."*

PRAYERS OF THANKSGIVING FOR USE WHEN HOLY COMMUNION IS NOT CELEBRATED 197–203

The prayer of thanksgiving begins with the same dialogue that introduces the great prayer of thanksgiving of the Lord's Supper. The dialogue is as follows:

197

The Lord be with you.

And also with you.

Lift up your hearts.

We lift them to the Lord.

Let us give thanks to the Lord our God.

It is right to give our thanks and praise.

On nonsacramental days, the prayer of thanksgiving may begin with this abbreviated dialogue:

198

Let us give thanks to the Lord our God.

It is right to give our thanks and praise.

One of the following prayers, or a similar prayer of thanksgiving, is then prayed, concluding with the Lord's Prayer.

199

We thank you, O God,
for you are gracious.
You have loved us from the beginning of time
and you have remembered us when we were in trouble.

Your mercy endures forever.

We thank you, O God,
for you came to us in Jesus Christ,
who has redeemed the world
and saved us from our sins.

Your mercy endures forever.

We thank you, O God,
for you send us your Holy Spirit,
to comfort us
and to lead us into all truth.

Your mercy endures forever. Amen.

Our Father . . .

200

O God,
creator of this pleasant world
and giver of all good things,
we thank you for our home on earth
and for the joy of living.
We praise you for your love in Jesus Christ,
who came to set things right,
who died rejected on the cross
and rose triumphant from the dead.
Because he lives, we live to praise you, our God forever.

**O God, who called us from death to life,
we give ourselves to you;
and with the church through all ages
we thank you for your saving love
in Jesus Christ our Lord. Amen.**

Our Father . . .

201

Almighty and merciful God,
from whom comes all good, and every perfect gift,
we praise you for your mercies,
for your goodness that has created us,
your grace that has sustained us,
your discipline that has corrected us,
your patience that has borne with us,
and your love that has redeemed us.
Help us to love you,
and to be thankful for all your gifts
by serving you and delighting to do your will,
through Jesus Christ our Lord.

Amen.

Our Father . . .

202

God of all mercies,
we give you humble thanks
for all your goodness and loving-kindness
to us and to all whom you have made.
We bless you for our creation, preservation,
and all the blessings of this life;
but above all for your immeasurable love
in the redemption of the world by our Lord Jesus Christ;
for the means of grace,
and for the hope of glory.
And, we pray,
give us such an awareness of your mercies,
that with truly thankful hearts
we may show forth your praise,
not only with our lips, but in our lives,
by giving up ourselves to your service,
and by walking before you
in holiness and righteousness all our days;
through Jesus Christ our Lord,
to whom, with you and the Holy Spirit,
be honor and glory throughout all ages.

Amen.

Our Father . . .

203

Holy God, we praise you.
Let the heavens be joyful,
and the earth be glad.

We bless you for creating the whole world,
for your promises to your people Israel,
and for the life we know in Jesus Christ your Son.

Born of Mary, he shares our life.
Eating with sinners, he welcomes us.
Leading his followers, he guides us.
Dying on the cross, he rescues us.
Risen from the dead, he gives new life.

Send us your Holy Spirit
that your people may become one.
Unite us in faith, inspire us to love,
encourage us with hope,
that, being made one with Christ,
we may be one with each other
and one in ministry to all the world,
until Christ comes in final victory.

We praise you, almighty Father,
through Christ your Son,
in the Holy Spirit.

Amen.

Our Father . . .

THE LORD'S PRAYER 204–208

204
As our Savior Christ has taught us,
we now pray:

205
And now,
with the confidence of the children of God,
let us pray:

206
Let us pray for God's rule on earth
as Jesus taught us:

207
Our Father in heaven,
hallowed be your name,
your kingdom come,
your will be done,
on earth as in heaven.
Give us today our daily bread.
Forgive us our sins
as we forgive those who sin against us.
Save us from the time of trial
and deliver us from evil.
For the kingdom, the power, and the glory are yours
now and forever. Amen.

208
Our Father, who art in heaven,
hallowed be thy name,
thy kingdom come,
thy will be done,
on earth as it is in heaven.
Give us this day our daily bread;
and forgive us our debts,
as we forgive our debtors;
and lead us not into temptation,
but deliver us from evil.
For thine is the kingdom,
and the power, and the glory, forever. Amen.

209

If the words of institution were not included in the great prayer of thanksgiving, the minister, standing before the people, says the following words (based on I Cor. 11:23–26 and Luke 22:19–20).

The minister breaks bread in the presence of the people, saying:

The Lord Jesus,
on the night of his arrest,
took bread,
and after giving thanks to God,
he broke it and said,
"This is my body, given for you.
Do this in remembrance of me."

The minister lifts the cup, saying:

In the same way,
he took the cup after supper, saying,
"This cup is the new covenant sealed in my blood.
Whenever you drink it,
do it in remembrance of me."

Every time you eat this bread and drink this cup,
you proclaim the death of the Lord, until he comes.

210

If the words of institution were included in the great prayer of thanksgiving, the following may be used (I Cor. 10:16, 17):

Because there is one loaf,
we, many as we are, are one body;
for it is one loaf of which we all partake.

Here the presiding minister takes the loaf and breaks it in full view of the congregation.

When we break the bread,
is it not a sharing in the body of Christ?

Here the minister lifts the cup.

When we give thanks over the cup,
is it not a sharing in the blood of Christ?

The minister then holds out both the bread and the cup to the people.

The gifts of God
for the people of God.

211

The bread may be broken in silence. The minister may then say:

The gifts of God
for the people of God.

"JESUS, LAMB OF GOD" 212–213

One of the following, or another version of "Jesus, Lamb of God," may be sung after the breaking of the bread or during the serving.

212
Jesus, Lamb of God:
have mercy on us.
Jesus, bearer of our sins:
have mercy on us.
Jesus, redeemer of the world:
give us your peace.

213
Lamb of God, you take away the sins of the world:
have mercy on us.
Lamb of God, you take away the sins of the world:
have mercy on us.
Lamb of God, you take away the sins of the world:
grant us peace.

WORDS AT THE GIVING OF THE BREAD AND WINE

214

The bread of heaven.

Amen.

The cup of salvation.

Amen.

215

Jesus Christ, the bread of heaven.

Amen.

Jesus Christ, the cup of salvation.

Amen.

216

The body of Christ, the bread of heaven.

Amen.

The blood of Christ, the cup of salvation.

Amen.

217

The body of Christ given for you.

Amen.

The blood of Christ shed for you.

Amen.

218

N ___________, the body of Christ, the bread of heaven.

Amen.

N ___________, the blood of Christ, the cup of salvation.

Amen.

PRAYERS AFTER COMMUNION 219–229

One of the following prayers may be offered by the minister or by all.

219

Bless the Lord, O my soul;

and all that is within me, bless God's holy name!

Bless the Lord, O my soul,

and forget not all God's benefits. *Ps. 103:1, 2*

220

Gracious God, you have made us one
with all your people in heaven and on earth.
You have fed us with the bread of life,
and renewed us for your service.
We give ourselves to you,
and ask that our daily living
may be part of the life of your kingdom.
May our love be your love
reaching out into the life of the world;
through Jesus Christ our Lord.

Amen.

221

Eternal God, we give you thanks for this holy mystery
in which you have given yourself to us.
Grant that we may go into the world
in the strength of your Spirit,
to give ourselves for others
in the name of Jesus Christ our Lord.

Amen.

222

Most loving God,
you have given us a share in the one bread and the one cup
and made us one with Christ.
Help us to bring your salvation and joy to all the world.
We ask this through Christ our Lord.

Amen.

223

O God,
you have so greatly loved us,
long sought us,
and mercifully redeemed us.
Give us grace
that in everything we may yield ourselves,
our wills and our works,
a continual thank-offering to you;
through Jesus Christ our Lord.

Amen.

224

God of grace,
you renew us at your table with the bread of life.
May this food strengthen us in love
and help us to serve you in each other.
We ask this in the name of Jesus the Lord.

Amen.

225

Loving God,
we thank you that you have fed us in this Sacrament,
united us with Christ,
and given us a foretaste of the heavenly banquet
in your eternal kingdom.
Send us out in the power of your Spirit
to live and work to your praise and glory.

Amen.

226

We thank you, O God,
that through Word and Sacrament
you have given us your Son
who is the true bread of heaven
and food of eternal life.
So strengthen us in your service
that our daily living may show our thanks,
through Jesus Christ our Lord.

Amen.

227
Eternal God,
you have graciously accepted us
as living members of your Son our Savior Jesus Christ,
and you have fed us with spiritual food
in the Sacrament of his body and blood.
Send us now into the world in peace,
and grant us strength and courage
to love and serve you with gladness and singleness of heart;
through Christ our Lord.

Amen.

228
You have given yourself to us, Lord;

now we give ourselves for others.

Your love has made us a new people;

as a people of love we will serve you with joy.

Your glory has filled our hearts;

help us to glorify you in all things. Amen.

229
Lord, now you let your servant go in peace;
your word has been fulfilled:
my own eyes have seen the salvation
which you have prepared in the sight of every people:
a light to reveal you to the nations
and the glory of your people Israel. *Luke 2:29–32*

CHARGES TO THE PEOPLE 230–239

A charge to the people may be said before or after the minister gives God's blessing. A ruling elder, a deacon, or the minister may give the charge when it follows the blessing.

230

Go out into the world in peace;
have courage;
hold on to what is good;
return no one evil for evil;
strengthen the fainthearted;
support the weak, and help the suffering;
honor everyone;
love and serve the Lord,
rejoicing in the power of the Holy Spirit.

I Cor. 16:13
II Tim. 2:1
Eph. 6:10
I Thess. 5:13–22
I Peter 2:17

231

Be watchful,
stand firm in your faith,
be courageous and strong.
Let all that you do be done in love.

I Cor. 16:13, 14

232

Whatever you do, in word or deed,
do everything in the name of the Lord Jesus,
giving thanks to God through him.

Col. 3:17

233

God has shown you what is good.
What does the Lord require of you
but to do justice,
and to love kindness,
and to walk humbly with your God?

Micah 6:8

234

Go forth in the name of the Lord.
This is God's charge:
to give our allegiance to Jesus Christ
and to love one another as he commanded.

I John 3:23

235
Go out into the world in peace.
Love the Lord your God
with all your heart,
with all your soul,
with all your mind.
This is the greatest commandment:
it comes first.

The second is like it:
Love your neighbor as yourself.

Everything in the law and the prophets
hangs on these two commandments. *Matt. 22:37–40*

While the following charges may be used either before or after the blessing, they are particularly appropriate when used after the blessing.

When the charge follows the blessing, the people may respond with "Thanks be to God." *From Easter Sunday through Pentecost Sunday,* "Alleluia, alleluia" *may be added.*

236
Go in peace to love and serve the Lord.

Thanks be to God. [Alleluia, alleluia.]

237
Go in peace to serve the Lord, in the name of Christ.

Thanks be to God. [Alleluia, alleluia.]

238
Let us go forth into the world,
rejoicing in the power of the Holy Spirit.

Thanks be to God. [Alleluia, alleluia.]

239
Let us bless the Lord.

Thanks be to God. [Alleluia, alleluia.]

240
The grace of our Lord Jesus Christ
and the love of God
and the fellowship of the Holy Spirit
be with you all. *II Cor. 13:14*

Amen.

241
The Lord bless you and keep you.
The Lord be kind and gracious to you.
The Lord look upon you with favor
and give you peace. *Num. 6:24–26*

Amen.

242
The peace of God, which passes all understanding,
keep your hearts and minds
in the knowledge and love of God,
and of God's Son Jesus Christ our Lord; *Phil. 4:7*
and the blessing of God almighty,
the Father, the Son, and the Holy Spirit,
remain with you always.

Amen.

243
May the God of peace
make you holy in every way
and keep your whole being—
spirit, soul, and body—
free from every fault
at the coming of our Lord Jesus Christ. *I Thess. 5:23*

Amen.

244
May the God of hope
fill you with all joy and peace in believing,
so that you may abound in hope
by the power of the Holy Spirit. *Rom. 15:13*

Amen.

245

The God of peace brought our Lord Jesus,
the great shepherd of the flock,
back again from the dead.
May God give you every good gift,
that you may do God's will.
May our God work within you
all that is pleasing in God's sight
through Jesus Christ.
Glory be to Jesus for ever and ever! *Heb. 13:20, 21*

Amen.

The following prayers may be used by worshipers for personal prayer after the dismissal.

246

Almighty God,
grant that the words we have heard this day with our ears
may be grafted onto our hearts through your grace,
that they may produce in us the fruit of a good life,
to the praise and honor of your name;
through Jesus Christ our Lord. Amen.

247

After Holy Communion

Almighty God,
you provide the true bread from heaven,
your Son, Jesus Christ our Lord.
Grant that we who have received the Sacrament of his body and blood
may abide in him
and he in us,
that we may be filled with the power of his endless life,
now and forever. Amen.

A COMMENTARY ON THE ORDER FOR THE SERVICE FOR THE LORD'S DAY

1
CONVICTIONS CONCERNING WORSHIP

Worship as praise and glorification of God is central to the life of any Reformed congregation. Whatever else may characterize the people of God, the weekly Lord's Day assembly for worship is the one predictable moment in their corporate obedience and self-dedication. Its predictability is significant. It will happen again. The community will *re*-assemble, at whatever cost. The Christian community, because of its priceless heritage, will greet the future in faith, hope, and love.[1]

The centrality of this repeated event in which the church manifests itself as church, to itself and to the world, suggests the seriousness with which the ordering of the event should be taken. As *The Directory for the Service of God* states: "Public worship need not follow prescribed forms. However, careless public worship may be both an offense to God and a stumbling block to the people."[2]

This proposed form for *The Service for the Lord's Day* seeks to provide a carefully considered structure for this weekly formative event in the life of God's people while respecting the liberty of congregations to shape their own liturgical life. Many options are suggested in the hope that they will not be confusing but liberating. This brief commentary explains why specific proposals are made.

Pastoral sensitivity is always to be exercised in adapting this order to any given congregation. Congregations rich in ethnic expressions of worship will bring their own cherished forms and styles, thereby reflecting the variety of ways the worship of God has taken root in various cultures. This diversity is respected in the flexibilitv incorporated in this order.

As an expression of the Reformed tradition, this order is designed to express three basic functions of worship: praise, proclamation, and presence. The praise or glorification of God has always been central in the Reformed heritage. At its heart is the proclamation of God's good news in Word and Sacrament. Wherever the Word is heard and the Sacraments are celebrated, God's Spirit is present to the community, and through the community to the world.

In worship, as in all God's dealings with people, the initiative lies with God. Nevertheless, public worship is at every point a human action. In this respect the community has its treasure "in earthen vessels" (II Cor. 4:7). What is done in worship can never escape the critical question of whether it "is rightly done, or whether it might not be done differently and better."[3] For this reason, *The Directory for the Service of God* assigns responsibility for what occurs in public worship to the session, so that worship may be given the care it requires.[4]

In the past decade other denominations have reexamined their worship practices. The order contained in this volume reflects the ecumenical consensus that has emerged while preserving the distinctive elements of our own heritage.

This proposed form for worship on the Lord's Day has been shaped by our theology, by positive ecumenical developments, and by the wisdom of Christian history. In this form the session may find a means of helping people to express and experience praise, proclamation, and presence in a way that gives honor and glory to God and leads the people of God to deeper faith and love.

Several convictions, implicit and explicit, have given particular form to this order. A liturgical order and text do not constitute a liturgy. A liturgy is an event that involves people and place, text and context. Nevertheless, this order with its suggested texts carries with it a series of convictions that should be considered in any evaluation or use. They reflect both Reformed and ecumenical experience. These convictions may be described as follows.

A. Liturgy and Life

A primary conviction holds that liturgy and life, worship and mission, are inseparable.[5] Reformed confessions historically have regarded the whole of Christian obedience as praise and worship. Particularly in the opening and closing rites of this order, significant connections are drawn between the liturgical gathering and the worldly obedience of the Christian and the church. The word "service" deliberately refers to both. While public worship occurs at designated times in particular places and consists of specific cultic actions, it is also part and parcel of daily life. It expresses not only our praise, prayer, confession, and thanksgiving but also our commitment to do God's will at all times and under all circumstances.

Another way to express this relatedness is to say that worship is inseparable from mission. Worshipers bring to the assembly their personal cares and concerns that the community may support them in prayer and sympathy. Then at the conclusion of worship they are dismissed to carry on Christ's mission in the world. Even at worship, the Christian community points beyond itself. "The ministry of the church to others is service to God, a response to grace, done in obedience to the will of God made known in Scripture."[6]

B. Word and Sacrament

A second conviction holds that Word and Sacrament form the normative pattern for the Sunday assembly. This affirmation has deep roots in the practice of the early church as well as in the work of the sixteenth-century Reformers. Calvin declared without qualification, "We ought always to provide that no meeting of the Church is held without the Word, prayer, the dispensation of the Supper, and alms."[7] His authority was Scripture and the practice of the early church.

Calvin was able to celebrate Holy Communion monthly in Strassburg, but only quarterly in Geneva. He augmented that schedule, however, by insisting that the Lord's Supper should be observed "three times a year generally, that is to say at Easter, Pentecost, and Christmas."[8]

The Directory for the Service of God specifies: "It is fitting to celebrate the Sacrament as frequently as each Lord's Day, and at least as often as quarterly. Observance should be regular enough that it is seen as a proper part of and not an addition to the worship of God."[9] To restore a more regular observance of the Lord's Supper will require educational effort and liturgical reform in many congregations. This order provides structures and texts for such an undertaking. Note the parallel sequences of the thanksgiving provided to set forth the "normative" pairing of Word and Sacrament even on Sundays when the Supper is not included. Use of the Christian annual calendar with its focal emphasis on Christmas-Epiphany and Easter-Pentecost is assumed. This calendar provides a multiplicity of occasions for celebrating the Sacrament.

There are pastoral as well as historical and theological reasons for celebrating the Sacrament as a normal Sunday practice. Protestant worship tends to be excessively intellectual and verbal. As a result, most Protestant worship is problematic to children, persons who experience hearing barriers, and those whose personal self-consciousness is more affective or feeling-oriented. The recovery of sacramental worship at its best could correct this imbalance. It would also bring us closer to other Christian traditions which—as did Calvin—encourage the faithful to communicate more frequently as well as to appreciate more fully the importance of preaching.

C. Freedom and Form

A third conviction is that worship, particularly in the Reformed tradition, should provide a judicious mixture of freedom and form, of structure and spontaneity. This would seem to be the counsel Paul gave when he said, "Do not forbid speaking in tongues; but all things should be done decently and in order" (I Cor. 14:39–40). While Presbyterians have always stressed order, they have often been short on spontaneity.

This proposed order for worship provides a pattern within which there is freedom to respond to the promptings of the Spirit. A variety of liturgical texts is included. Alternate location of some parts of the order is suggested. There are spaces for silence, for individual responses, for expressions of concern, and for artistic offerings. An outline of the great prayer of thanksgiving, as well as full texts, is provided. Other Bible translations may be used for the liturgical text where they clarify confusing passages or suggest fresh insights. A variety of musical styles and forms is suggested to allow for broader ethnic and cultural contributions.

Liturgical directions are phrased in a way that avoids both mandatory language and total permissiveness. Freedom and form are not to be pitted against each other; rather, they are mutually supportive. Lack of structure does not necessarily create freedom; neither does freedom do away with form, "for God is not a God of confusion but of peace" (I Cor. 14:33). Without structure, freedom can degenerate into license. Form enables freedom to be truly freedom.

D. People and Participation

Another conviction, both Reformed and ecumenical, affirms the people's role as participants in the liturgy. "The priesthood of all believers" was a cardinal principle of the Reformation. To enhance the people's participation in worship, the Scriptures were translated into the vernacular, and worship was conducted in the language they spoke. This order seeks to include the people as active participants in the service.

Contemporary English is used as expressively as possible. A wide variety of musical, graphic, and ceremonial expressions, dialogue, unison prayers and affirmations, and a plurality of leaders is assumed in this order. Different individuals as well as the whole assembled people of God may participate in the service in a variety of ways.

Most congregations prepare a leaflet as an aid to the people's participation. What needs to be included in such a leaflet? Where the congregation uses a resource such as *The Worshipbook, The Book of Common Worship,* or the booklet for the pew which may be used with this order, only the variables—such as the hymn numbers, the readings, the location of the people's prayers and responses to be used in the liturgy on that day—need appear. Even when a service book is not used, only portions for the people need be provided.

It is not necessary to provide worshipers with the entire sequence of the service. As long as the leaders of worship are adept and discreet in referring to these aids, doing so should not be distracting, any more than is referring to a specific hymn number.

It is of great value for the congregation to know from memory the recurring portions of the liturgy. C. S. Lewis once said that we are not dancing until we no longer have to count the steps. So also, when we know by heart the common parts of the liturgy we are less self-conscious about our worship and are enabled to participate with greater spontaneity and freedom. The congregation might therefore be encouraged to memorize those portions of the liturgy which are in common use in Christian worship.

The best way to begin is to recover the use of the little word "Amen." "Amen" is a Hebrew word meaning "So be it!" It is a word that belongs to the people and has been used from ancient times as the people's assent to prayer (I Chron. 16:36; Neh. 8:6; Ps. 106:48; I Cor. 14:16). When the people fervently add "Amen" to prayers offered by a leader of worship, they actively participate in the prayers and embrace them as their own. The recovery of this practice will greatly help a congregation move from being passive listeners in worship to becoming active participants.

Other basic portions of the liturgy to know from memory include: (*a*) the response to a greeting such as "The Lord be with you," which is "And also with you" (19–21); (*b*) the response after a reading from

Scripture, "Thanks be to God" (116–117); (*c*) the words for the exchange of the peace (98–100); (*d*) the Nicene Creed (135) and the Apostles' Creed (136); (*e*) the people's portions of the great prayer of thanksgiving, namely, the dialogue that begins the prayer (183–189, 197), the "Holy, holy, holy Lord" (191), the memorial acclamation (193), and the concluding "Amen"; and (*f*) the modern text for the Lord's Prayer (207).

When these are known, others may be added, such as the "Lord, have mercy" (83), a response to words of pardon (89 or 90), the "Glory to God in the highest" (92), the words introducing and concluding the Gospel reading (113 and 118), intercession responses (144, 145, 147), "Jesus, Lamb of God" (212 or 213), and responses to the charge (236–239).

Outside of the liturgical event itself there are other ways to encourage participation. One is to have a worship committee with representatives from the session and the congregation to help plan aspects of the service. This practice not only enriches the liturgy but also expands and deepens the members' understanding of it.

Another way to broaden participation and enrich worship is to organize a discussion group centering upon the Scriptures to be read and interpreted in worship. To study together the passages that the preaching will interpret can greatly assist both preacher and hearers to discover the connections between God's Word and today's issues.

E. The Formative Role of Scripture

Another conviction recognizes the formative role of the language of Scripture. This order of service relies on the inspired books for its major moments. Both the greeting and the dismissal are based on Biblical texts. This admittedly differs from some contemporary practice where freely composed material is casually used, particularly at the opening of the service.[10] Biblical texts are also used in the call to confession, the affirmation of faith, the invitation to Holy Communion, words at the giving of bread and wine in Communion, the final charge to the congregation, and the blessing.

Most important, perhaps, this order integrates Scripture lessons, psalms, sermon, and intercessory prayers in the section entitled "Proclaim God's Word." These elements, always highly regarded by Presbyterians, have become liturgically scattered, thus obscuring their interrelatedness. The sequence is important; the readings and the psalm (which is properly corporate praise rather than simply another reading) precede the sermon. The prayers, which arise from the preaching as well as from the concerns of the people, come after the sermon.

Further, it is recommended that the readings from Scripture follow the lectionary, thereby giving comprehensive attention to both Testaments. This practice supports the declaration of the *Directory* that "over a period of time the people shall hear the full message of Scripture."[11] The use of the lectionary also has implications for the preacher. Allowing "such latitude as may be proper in varying situations," a set order of readings is designed "to assure that the fullness of God's Word is declared."[12]

This seriousness about Scripture will be seen in the various directions in this order that musical texts and the Sacraments of Baptism and the Lord's Supper themselves be related to Biblical proclamation. The liturgical texts also show a marked preference for Biblical language and metaphor.

The Christian calendar also stresses the centrality of Scripture. Its purpose is to ensure that the community annually celebrates the incarnation of Christ (Advent-Christmas-Epiphany), and his resurrection (Lent-Easter-Pentecost).[13] The ecumenical lectionary provides Biblical readings for these celebrations and for the intervening Sundays ("after Epiphany" and "after Pentecost"). Thus the calendar provides a means for dealing with Scripture systematically and Christologically.

F. Contemporary and Traditional Language

Finally, this order makes use of both traditional and contemporary resources. The rich heritage of the past is not rejected in an effort to speak relevantly to our time, nor cherished simply because it is old.

The editing of the great prayers of thanksgiving is illustrative. Prayer A (183, page 88) is a revision of a prayer from *The Worshipbook.* It provides for optional seasonal variations and the use of the words of institution as part of the prayer. A memorial acclamation is added. Prayer B (184, page 98) was written for this order. It follows the trinitarian structure, using generic language. Prayer C (185, page 102) is a revision of the much-loved text from *The Book of Common Worship.* The words of institution have been added as an option, its language has been made contemporary, and a memorial acclamation is included. Prayer D (186, page 106) is a translation of the oldest extant eucharistic prayer in the Western church, that of Hippolytus (ca. A.D. 215). Prayer E (187, page 108) is an adaptation of the fourth-century Alexandrine Liturgy of St. Basil. Prayer F (188, page 111) is an ecumenical prayer prepared by the Commission on Worship of the Consultation on Church Union. Prayer G (189, page 116) combines a number of texts from John Calvin, with opening dialogue and memorial acclamation added. Prayer H (190, page 118) is a new prayer. This brief prayer is intended for use when Holy Communion is celebrated in the home or hospital, or in other informal situations. It was not prepared for use with congregations on the Lord's Day.

Liturgical texts that are the common ecumenical heritage, such as the Lord's Prayer (207), the Apostles' Creed (136), and the Nicene Creed (135), are given in the most recent versions prepared by the International Consultation on English Texts (see also 83, 84, 86, 92, 191, 197, 212, 213, 229; and the opening dialogue and "Holy, holy, holy Lord" in 183–190). The consultation was composed of Protestant and Roman Catholic representatives from twenty countries where English is spoken. Its work is a remarkable achievement in Christian unity. The result is that a common text is appearing in the service books of most churches in English-speaking countries. The ICET texts in this resource supersede those in *The Worshipbook.*

In preparing this *Service for the Lord's Day*, particular care was taken in regard to the use of generic language. In the past, masculine terms and pronouns were used as generic without challenge. Today, however, many believe such usage is discriminatory and exclusive. Problems arise in two particular areas: (1) language concerning the people of God, and (2) language concerning God. The first problem was addressed by a joint committee of The United Presbyterian Church in the U.S.A. and the Presbyterian Church in the U.S., which reported to their General Assemblies in Louisville in 1974.[14] The second was addressed by the Advisory Council on Discipleship and Worship of The United Presbyterian Church, reporting to the 1978 General Assembly, and by the Council on Theology and Culture, reporting to the 1980 General Assembly of the Presbyterian Church U.S.[15] The recommendations made in these studies were followed in as responsible a manner as seemed possible. Care was also taken to avoid language that reflects an ethnic or ageist bias or discriminates against those with handicapping conditions. The preliminary drafts were circulated widely with such an agenda in mind. It is hoped that this order will be seen and experienced as reflecting these concerns.

2
A PRESBYTERIAN ORDER FOR WORSHIP

This order for the Service for the Lord's Day (pages 11–26) consists of four successive actions:

Assemble in God's Name
Proclaim God's Word
Give Thanks to God
Go in God's Name

At the heart of the order is the classic pairing of Word and Sacrament. Surrounding these central events are the briefer rites for meeting and parting. These outer rites provide transitions between the community's involvement in the secular order and its own gathering as God's people ordered by Word and Sacrament. This structure should always be kept in mind in planning the Lord's Day service.

Any serious social gathering requires acceptable ways of beginning and ending. The Christian community recognizes the importance of this. God's people are no less a people when separated from one another in mission than when assembled in worship, and no more a people when assembled for prayer, praise, and communion than when they are scattered in pursuit of peace and justice.

Every gathering of Christians may be described as the gracious act of God whereby we share the mutuality and interdependence that is God's order for creation. In worship this is symbolized by the exchange of the peace. Whenever Christians part, symbolized in worship by the dismissal "Go in peace," they leave the assembly to witness and serve in friendly or unfriendly contexts. Individually and as the body of believers, Christians in the secular world express the purpose of their assemblies as they await the coming of the Day of the Lord, "encouraging one another, and all the more as you see the Day drawing near" (Heb. 10:25).

Sound historical reasons support this fourfold pattern as the basis for the Sunday service of worship.

A. Origins of the Fourfold Pattern

It is impossible to derive from the New Testament a full or normative description of Christian worship. There are hints in words, hymns, and phrases scattered throughout the apostolic writings, and there are brief treatises on the proper conduct of worship, particularly in I Corinthians 11–14. Paul's teaching on "spiritual worship" in Romans 12 clearly reflects the gathered and scattered phases of the Christian's life. Traces of early rites of Word and Sacrament may be found in Luke 24:13–35 and Acts 20:7–11.

The *Didache*, a first-century document, gives directions for a Lord's Supper associated with a full meal. It contains references to the new covenant and Jesus' expected immediate return. Justin Martyr (ca. A.D. 150) and Hippolytus (ca. A.D. 215) provide the earliest evidence of the order of worship followed in the Western church. A weekly Word and Sacrament event appears to have been the norm in the writings of Justin.

The pattern for worship that emerged in the postapostolic period consisted first of a liturgy of the Word, which included Scripture readings, a sermon, and intercessory prayers. This was followed by the celebration of the Supper, supplemented by a collection and the distribution of the elements to those who were absent.

Hippolytus in his *Apostolic Tradition* provides some details of this order and gives the first full text of a eucharistic prayer.

Concerning the assembling, "we know that until the end of the fourth century, in both East and West, the service formally began, after a call to order by the bishop or deacon, with the reading of the lessons." A source from the West dating from the late seventh century informs us that the readings were "preceded by four distinct items, the Introit, the *Kyries*, the *Gloria* and the Collect."[16]

In the East the opening rites were the responsibility of the deacon. The deacon functioned throughout worship much like a combination cantor-cheerleader. The deacon might be seen as the people's cleric and was pastorally closest to the congregation. Charged to care for widows, orphans, and the needy, the deacon had responsibilities that put him close to the people. It was of great significance, therefore, that this person ministered at the moments of meeting and parting, and throughout encouraged the people to sing, pray, and respond. At the opening of the service the deacon led a litany of intercessions for the whole world to which the people responded, "Lord, have mercy." Only that response remains in the Western rite. The deacon in the East also dismissed the people after the priest had given the blessing. This practice is being recovered in some modern orders. In this order, as an alternate practice, it is suggested (page 132) that a ruling elder or a deacon may give the charge following the blessing given by the minister.

B. Reform

The sixteenth-century Reformers, especially in Geneva, drew upon the New Testament and patristic tradition in forming their service of public worship. Calvin's prayer books carried in their title "the customs of the ancient church."[17] To a large degree this recovery of early church practice was the basis for his recasting of the Roman rite.

What new form did the Reformers give to the liturgy of the medieval church? If the Lord's Supper was celebrated, it followed these four stages: (1) assembly in praise and confession; (2) the reading and preaching of the Word, followed by a creed; (3) prayer and Communion; and (4) post-Communion prayer, praise, and blessing. If the Sacrament was not included in the order, only those elements pertaining to the Supper were changed.

This ancient pattern was displaced, however, by the Westminster Directory for Worship (1645). The Directory, James H. Nichols reminds us, represents "the liturgical crosscurrents within the Puritanism of that time and must be studied from that point of view. It is also the indispensable base point from which to grasp the development of the worship of English-speaking Presbyterians, Congregationalists, and Baptists for the three centuries since that day."[18]

This Directory was really not a service book at all, "but a manual for the discretionary use of ministers."[19] It assumed that the sermon would be the climax of the service, followed only by a prayer, a psalm or hymn, and the benediction. The general prayers of intercession, supplication, and thanksgiving preceded the sermon. Thus the historic structure was set aside except on Sacrament Sunday. On Sundays when the Sacrament was observed, the words of institution from I Corinthians 11 were to be read. The elements, set apart by prayer and thanksgiving, were distributed, and an offering was taken for the poor. When the Westminster Directory was adopted by the General Assembly of 1788, this became the accepted pattern for American Presbyterianism. Thus a structural difference between sacramental and nonsacramental Sundays came to characterize Presbyterian worship. The nonsacramental order became the norm.

Only when the United Presbyterian Directory for Worship was revised in 1961 and the service book portion of *The Worshipbook* appeared in 1970 were the Genevan and patristic precedents recovered. This present order builds upon that restoration. This is not to diminish the importance of the sermon, but to place it in its historic context, paired with the Sacrament of Holy Communion and surrounded by rites of assembly and dismissal. Even on nonsacramental Sundays the sermon is followed by prayers of intercession, an offering, and an act of thanksgiving.

Always in the Reformed tradition the people's offering is regarded as an act of thanksgiving. The prayer at the presentation of the offering is most properly a prayer of thanksgiving that emphasizes the grace of God. Giving is in response to God's boundless grace and mercy. Christian giving is thanksgiving. The prayer therefore should center upon the praises of God rather than upon the givers or their gifts.

C. Renewal

Apostolic, patristic, and Reformation precedent provide historical support for the pattern of Sunday worship provided in this order. However, the situations confronting the church in ancient and Reformation times were not identical with those that confront us today That difference needs to be considered when adapting the old rites for our own use. Nevertheless, except for serious reasons, that heritage ought not to be set aside. The disputes and preoccupations of the Westminster Assembly are not ours today and should not be allowed to separate us from the great and ancient traditions to which Calvin made appeal.

With the recovery of the Word-Sacrament shape as normative, we children of Calvin rejoin the ecumenical tradition and orient ourselves toward the coming of the unity of the church and the rule of Christ. We believe that in the recovery of Word and Sacrament we are being open to the movement of the Spirit in today's church, and we pray that, through such reordering of our worship life, God will more powerfully renew our faith.

3
THE PURPOSE OF THE PATTERN

Each part of the fourfold pattern of the Service for the Lord's Day fulfills a separate and distinctive purpose. At the same time, the four parts of the order are integrally related actions in one unified service of worship. Each will be discussed in turn, together with the reasons for it.

A. Assemble in God's Name

The opening and closing portions of the order serve a similar purpose. As transitions into and out of the "Word-Sacrament celebration," they are what sociologists call "threshold" moments. The entry rite of assembling in God's name is designed to move both worshipers and ministers from their worldly context into the assembly where the Scripture and Sacrament are central.

The opening includes informal and communal sharing, silence, music, praise, and confession. Too often the first three are done simultaneously and the latter two are not always balanced. To avoid the conflict of conversation, silent prayer, and organ (or instrumental) music, it is suggested that these be done in sequence. Praise and confession are paired and completed with the peace, as expressive of reconciliation. A joyful response of praise follows.

In the opening, the people are reminded of God's gracious acts. They respond with praise and confession of sin and are reassured of God's mercy. They are now ready to hear the proclamation of God's Word.

B. Proclaim God's Word

Central in worship in the Reformed tradition is the proclamation of the good news of God in the midst of that community formed by the good news. Believing that "the one sufficient revelation of God is Jesus Christ, . . . to whom the Holy Spirit bears unique and authoritative witness through the Holy Scriptures,"[20] we must take the Bible seriously.

Consequently, at this point the major focus is upon the Bible. In the Church of Scotland, in anticipation of this moment, the Bible is carried in at the beginning of the service and reverently placed upon the pulpit or lectern. Such a visual sign can add significance to the opening "greeting."

The Bible is often not given the central role it deserves, and a neglect of systematic Biblical teaching results. This order seeks to recover the centrality of God's Word in worship. It offers four proposals to this end. First, it recommends that there be three readings from the Bible in each service—Old Testament, Epistle (or Acts during the Easter season), and Gospel.

Secondly, it proposes that these readings be chosen in reference to a lectionary, which is "an ordered system of selected readings appointed for liturgical use on specific occasions in the church year, thus presupposing a calendar."[21] This is in keeping with the sixteenth-century concern, based on the example of the early church, that the reading of Scripture and its exposition rely upon the wisdom of the church. A lectionary represents the considered wisdom of the church regarding both the Christian calendar and the canon of Scripture. Use of a lectionary need not inhibit a minister's freedom, for local circumstances should be respected and readings can be substituted. Nevertheless, a fundamental commitment to such a systematic approach to the entire Bible enables the congregation to study God's Word, assists those responsible for the music to relate it to the themes of the day, and gives the preacher options in selecting sermon subjects well in advance of a given Sunday. A wealth of homiletical and exegetical resources associated with the lectionary are available for sermon planning. Furthermore, there is great symbolic significance in congregations everywhere, of many different denominations, using the same Scripture texts week by week.

The use of the three-year, three-lesson lectionary permits the books of the Bible to speak on their own terms. Over the three years, the Synoptic Gospels are read in a semicontinuous manner. John is read at Christmas and Lent-Easter. Frequently the epistles are read in sequence for a series of Sundays. The new ecumenical revision of the lectionary extends this principle to the Old Testament readings "after Pentecost." This semicontinuous principle is important in that it recovers for us the most ancient principle of liturgical reading of the Scripture, the *lectio continua*. Thus, the lectionary provides many advantages for returning the Scriptures to the central place they have historically held in the tradition of the Reformers.[22]

In the third place, this order suggests that the congregation participate by singing hymns, spiritual songs, and psalms, and by the use of anthems between the Scripture lessons. The singing of psalms as an act of praise is a very important tradition. The Psalter was meant to be sung. For a very long time Presbyterians were known for their singing of the psalms. The Psalter provides a compendium of texts that is both God's Word to humanity and, liturgically, humanity's word to God. Dietrich Bonhoeffer said that in this prayerbook of the Bible we learn not only what God has to say to us but also what God wants to hear from us. "The Psalms are given to us to this end, that we may learn to pray them in the name of Jesus Christ."[23]

Fourthly, concrete ways are proposed in which the congregation not only hears the Word of God read and proclaimed but also responds to that proclamation. This order suggests a variety of responses to the reading and preaching of the Word. A hymn, or other music, may be sung relating either to the sermon or to that which follows. Baptism or the ordinances of commissioning (confirmation), marriage, ordination, healing, reconciliation, or burial may be included. An invitation to commitment may frequently be given. Prayers for the world, the church, the nation, the community, the congregation, and those in need should be offered. These prayers follow the preaching in order to be shaped and guided by it.

The offering then follows. The offering is also part of the people's response to the Word. Historically it is related to the Eucharist. In the early church, at the beginning of the liturgy, people brought food and gifts to be given to the poor and for use in the Eucharist. The deacons took bread and wine from among these gifts for use in the Sacrament. When later in the service the Lord's table was prepared, the bread and wine earlier set aside were brought to the table.[24] This order of service in this book suggests that the Lord's table be prepared while the gifts are gathered from the people.

The center of this part of the order is the reading and interpretation of the Biblical lessons. We are then led to responding and offering, for which prayer is essential. God's Word does not return to God empty (Isa. 55:11).

C. Give Thanks to God

The purpose of the third major portion of the service, that of giving thanks to God, is the visible and tangible proclamation of the good news of God in the midst of the community that has been assembled by the power and ministry of the Word. Prayer now moves to the center. The Heidelberg Catechism states that prayer is necessary "because it is the chief part of the gratitude which God requires of us, and because God will give his grace and Holy Spirit only to those who sincerely beseech him in prayer without ceasing, and who thank him for these gifts."[25] So also in this order, grateful thanksgiving is regarded as the summit of Christian worship and the shape of the Christian life.

Here, too, we claim our Jewish roots. A basic form of Jewish prayer is blessing, or praise. The most familiar of Jewish blessings is the praise addressed to God at the time of the meal: "Blessed are you, O Lord our God, ruler of the universe, who bring forth bread from the earth." This blessing formula could refer not only to God's provision of bread but to almost anything else in creation.

Christian worship is in a sense an expansion of this pattern, to bless or praise God for what God has done and to seek God's continued providence in the future. So this order for worship on the Lord's Day begins with praise, continues with the proclamation of God's mighty acts as recounted in Scripture, engages us in petition, opens out into praise and thanksgiving, and then sends us into our mission in the world.

In this movement, this order assumes weekly Communion as normative. It does not simply advocate more frequent sacramental practice. The purpose is not just to have *many* Communion services, but to recover the historic purpose both of Sacrament and of worship, namely, the thankful proclamation of the mighty deeds of God, whose acts culminate in the death and resurrection of Christ, of which the Supper has always been the great sign.

In practice, however, the emphasis of the Supper too often falls on Christ's death rather than his resurrection. The result is that the service becomes a solemn meditation upon the cross, human sin, and guilt. The remembrance becomes anything but thankful. For many believers it therefore seems strange to celebrate the Supper at Christmas or Easter, and unbearable to observe it each Lord's Day. The Sacrament has a richness and theological breadth that this order seeks to recover. Four proposals are offered.

First, the emphasis of the Supper should always be on praise and thanksgiving. Eucharist, the ancient title for the Lord's Supper, means "thanksgiving" and is closely related to the New Testament word for grace. The Sacrament was seen as a grateful celebration of grace. Remembrance is not thereby neglected, but is placed in its proper context. The words for "remember" in both Hebrew and Greek include a sense of joyful and grateful participation in the present reality of the events that are recalled. The Lord's Supper is the "joyful feast of the people of God." The remembered events for which thanks is given include not only the last supper and death of the Lord, but also the resurrection of Christ and those meals Jesus had with his disciples thereafter, as well as the promise of the great Messianic banquet of the kingdom of God (Luke 22).

Remembrance as thanksgiving is secured by the regular use of a prayer of thanksgiving as the central feature of this part of the service. Whether it is a prayer such as those included in this resource, or is extemporized, it should be a prayer that praises God, remembers Christ's death and resurrection, and seeks the presence of the Holy Spirit. After that, only the Lord's Prayer could be considered a fitting climax and summation.

Secondly, the Lord's Supper should be reunited with the Lord's Day (Acts 20:7). Sunday is the Lord's Day (Rev. 1:10), because it is the day on which Christians celebrate Christ's resurrection.[26] Long before Easter emerged as a special Sunday to celebrate the resurrection, the weekly gathering on the first day was the time for Christians to assemble in recognition of Christ's rising from the grave. So also, the Lord's Supper is a resurrection feast since every celebration of the Eucharist has occurred after the resurrection. The meals Jesus shared with his followers in his appearances after his resurrection have formed the meaning of the Eucharist just as much as has the Last Supper.[27]

Since the resurrection is the essential meaning of both Lord's Day and Lord's Supper, the reunion of both will reinforce for the event and the day the centrality of the Lord's resurrection. It might be argued that the divorce of the two has contributed to the Supper becoming more of a Good Friday event than an Easter event, and the Lord's Day becoming more a Sabbath than a first-day celebration of resurrection.

Two strategies are proposed for our recovery of the Lord's Day Eucharist. The first is that on Sundays when the Sacrament is not celebrated the service remains the same, only those portions being omitted that pertain to receiving the bread and the cup.

The second strategy is to use the Christian calendar. The principal festivals of that cycle are particularly appropriate occasions for celebrating the Sacrament: First Sunday of Advent, Christmas Eve, Christmas Day, Epiphany, Baptism of the Lord, Transfiguration, First Sunday of Lent, Maundy Thursday, Easter Vigil, Easter Day and each Sunday of the Easter season, Pentecost, World Communion Sunday, and All Saints' Day.

As congregations associate the Sacrament with these various festivals, a readiness will be created to move toward a weekly pattern. Furthermore, the Sacrament will be associated with the Gospel story rather than with the secular calendar, such as the first Sunday of each quarter or each month.

The third proposal is to provide more opportunities for the congregation to participate in the Sacrament. Emphasis on the communal nature of the Sacrament will correct what many perceive to be a privatizing and individualizing of the service. Therefore, this order highlights the meal aspects of the Sacrament: preparing the table, breaking the bread and pouring the wine, the serving, and the spoken and sung participation of all. The exchange of peace is also an option before or after Communion, thus forming a link between the Sacrament and a sense of community.

A greater sense of participation may be achieved also by the way the physical elements are prepared and shared. The use of a common cup and a loaf of bread is recommended, and this may lead to the Reformed custom of going to the table. Such practices have been found appealing to children and young people. Worship that is participatory, communal, and physical speaks more effectively to younger members of the community. In recent years, Presbyterians have discovered that sacramental worship is not solely an adult event. Participation in the Supper is a baptismal right. The Jewish Passover, an ancestor of the Supper, requires the presence of children. Sacramental worship is often more accessible to children than preaching usually is.

The fourth proposal for recovering the significance of the Sacrament is to emphasize the concrete connection between the Word made visible in the Sacrament and the Christian's daily life. This is expressed in the final section.

D. Go in God's Name

The concluding rite complements the opening rite. Those who have assembled in God's name now go in God's name. All that has happened in the assembly by way of praise, confession, proclamation, prayer, and thanksgiving is now, in the final moments of worship, directed toward daily praise and dedicated obedience in the common life.

The One who is present in the breaking of bread is present with us as we return to life in the secular order. The service of thanks having ended, the service of work now begins. The rite of dismissal, however brief, alerts the congregation to the fact that worship is not a retreat from the world but, rather, strengthens the church for life in the world. The Lord's Day service is the indispensable event by which the church is identified with its Lord and sent to identify with the Lord's world in its daily life.

To underscore this, the dismissal includes both charge and blessing. The people are admonished to go forth "in peace to love and serve the Lord" and are given a blessing, or benediction, in words from Scripture. The effect of this blessing is to sign the congregation with the divine name, the name in which we are baptized and by which we live and serve. We are thus reminded of who we are and to whom we belong. As we go forth, we go assured of God's gracious word that makes possible our fulfilling the charge.

If there is a second offering, it may be received as the people leave, since that is the direction of the giving and subsequent self-giving of the community, even as it is the content of the dismissal. This is in keeping with rites of the early church in which this missional reorientation was accomplished by an offering for the poor and sending the deacons to commune with those who were absent. A spoken dismissal by the deacon, as brief as "Go in peace," alerted the people to their discipleship. In this same spirit some contemporary orders include the parish and communal announcements in the dismissal.

Because of the festive character of worship and all Christian praise and service, it is proposed that congregational song begin this portion of the service and that organ or other instrumental music conclude it.

4
LEADING THE LORD'S DAY SERVICE

What is done in the weekly Lord's Day assembly of God's people deserves to be purposefully ordered and theologically informed. How it is done deserves equal care and understanding. The comments that follow are intended to explain and interpret the directions in *The Service for the Lord's Day*. The four parts of the pattern and the components of each part will be discussed as they occur.

A. Assemble in God's Name

Gathering

A variety of suggestions are included in this order (page 15) as appropriate to include in the gathering of the people. Leaders will include what is appropriate in the particular congregation. The following is recommended.

As the people gather they "may informally greet one another" (page 15). People who belong to a community quite naturally greet one another when they meet. Such informal conversation should not be either repressed or suppressed. It should not, however, continue indefinitely, for this is not the reason for their assembling.

Musical numbers at the opening and close of a service of worship are an integral part of the service. If they have been purposefully selected and carefully prepared, they deserve a reverent hearing by the congregation. Avoid using music as a time filler while the people gather.

When the designated hour has come for the service to begin, the congregation is alerted by some visual or aural sign, such as the ringing of the church bell, the bringing in of the Bible, the silent entrance of the choir, or the worship leader's going to the Lord's table.

"A leader welcomes the people with a greeting based on those in the New Testament epistles" (page 15). A well-chosen Biblical text (19–25) is a far more fitting way to begin the worship of almighty God than to say "Good morning" and make some casual comments.

After the Biblical greeting, parish announcements may be made. However, it may be more appropriate for announcements to be made at the end of the service as the people move out into the activities of the day and week. This is also a time to rehearse new hymns or parts of the liturgy with which the congregation is not familiar. If announcements and a rehearsal are included, care must be taken to prevent this preliminary time from becoming protracted.

Following the greeting (and announcements and rehearsal, if included), the leader may say, "Let us worship God." The congregation is now ready to give silent reverent attention to organ or other instrumental music that has been chosen with the season or Biblical texts in mind. All can now listen in that climate of prayer and meditation that so many regard as an essential part of the beginning of worship. Prayers (1–11) and other aids for meditation (18) may be provided for personal use by the worshipers in preparation for worship by the whole assembly.

Call to Worship

At this point the community enters upon its particular priesthood, the offering of praise and adoration. "Sentences of Scripture . . . are spoken or read responsively" (page 15; texts 26–51). The Psalter is a useful source for these sentences.[28]

Praise and Adoration

Next follows a hymn, or psalm, or spiritual song. All these options should be taken seriously. The long tradition of singing psalms should not be neglected. A hymn of praise is always appropriate. Churches with a particular ethnic or cultural background have their own powerful opening songs that should be sung.

If the choir is not in place, this is the time for the processional. A processional adds to the drama of assembling and might include the leaders of worship. However, processionals and recessionals deprive the congregation of the choir's assistance in two of the hymns since, in the words of the late Erik Routley, the choir "arrives late and leaves early."

After the congregational praise, a prayer of adoration can be prayed (as in *The Book of Common Worship* [1946] tradition), although this may be superfluous following the Scriptural sentences and hymn of praise. The opening prayers that are provided (52–63) may be most useful when confession of sin does not follow. The collect for the day is an appropriate alternative.

Confession of Sin

A number of denominational rites move directly to the Scripture readings and preaching, with confession being a separate event or brief rite immediately preceding the service itself. The Reformed tradition has ordinarily included the confession of sin in the service itself, where it has occurred in at least two different places: at this point in relation to the acts of praise and adoration, or after the sermon in preparation for the Sacrament. This order provides for either use.

It may be argued that the confession of sin need not be included on each Lord's Day. For example, one could conclude that since Lent is a time of penitence in preparing for Easter, confession of sin might be included during Lent but suspended during the Easter season. This would be in keeping with the Council of Nicaea, which declared that penitential rites were inappropriate during the great and joyful fifty days from Easter to Pentecost.[29] Since each Sunday is a celebration of the resurrection, one might further question the appropriateness of confession for the Lord's Day. It should be noted, however, that the inclusion of confession in Reformed rites results from historical roots, primarily the laying aside of private confession. Rites that do not include confession in the Lord's Day service provide for it at other times, most notably in daily services not intended for Sunday, or in private confession. Since Presbyterians ordinarily do not have daily communal worship, or a special rite of reconciliation, the confession of sin remains in this order as normative.

When confession is included in the first portion of the service, the following is proposed. The leader should stand near the table or among the people, rather than at the pulpit or lectern. It is preferable for the congregation either to kneel or stand. Although anyone may lead this portion of the service, the declaration of pardon is spoken by a minister of the Word.[30]

The order provides for (*a*) a call to confession in the words of Scripture (64–73); (*b*) silence (at least 15 seconds); (*c*) a unison prayer (74–82) or a psalm or musical selection; (*d*) silence or a penitential setting of "Lord, have mercy" (83–86); (*e*) Scriptural words of pardon spoken by a minister (87–91); (*f*) a spoken or sung response; and (*g*) the exchange of the peace (98–100), if not done elsewhere in the service. The simplest version of the sequence would be the call, the prayer, and words of pardon.

The inclusion here of the exchange of the peace is to recover its relation to mutual reconciliation and also to discourage its becoming an unfortunate interruption of worship for lighthearted camaraderie. The peace is a responsive act, and in order that it not become an interruption in the movement of the service, it is best exchanged by persons near one another rather than in a general rushing about by all. The tendency for the peace to dissolve into casual expressions of friendliness will thereby be avoided and the symbolic character of this action will be preserved.

If the people stand for confession, this means that they have been standing since the sentences and opening song. This is not inappropriate and provides a helpful psychological encouragement to keep this section brief. It also serves as an expressive shift of attitude as all then sit for the proclamation of God's Word, the second stage of this order.

B. Proclaim God's Word

Prayer

A prayer for illumination (101–111) is an appropriate entry into the reading and hearing of God's Word. The theological basis for such a prayer is stated in the words of John Calvin: "Our conviction of the truth of Scripture must be derived from a higher source than human conjectures, judgments, or reasons; namely the secret testimony of the Spirit."[31]

For those who follow the lectionary, the prayer for the day is suggested.[32] The prayers for the day relate to the seasons of the church year and the readings appointed for the day. If the prayer for the day is regularly used as the opening prayer, a prayer for illumination is said here. This prayer should be said by the person who will read the first lesson—from the place where the lesson will be read—and the people should respond with "Amen."

Readings

The public reading of Scripture is an important part of Christian worship. Paul admonished Timothy to "attend to the public reading of scripture" (I Tim. 4:13). Because of the importance of the public reading of Scripture, it is recommended that all three lessons in the lectionary be read. Even if a lesson is not used in the sermon, it has value in and of itself as a reading from God's Word appointed for the day. It can contribute to our edification even if it is not used in the sermon. The traditional sequence of reading is Old Testament, Epistle, and Gospel. This may be changed, depending on which lesson is emphasized.

Lay members of the congregation, properly prepared, may share in the reading. They will need guidance as to which translation to read and how to read it so that its meaning may be effectively expressed.

Readings should usually take place at the lectern or the pulpit, the space set aside for the proclamation of the Word. Many church buildings lack the acoustics to make hearing possible when the lessons are read from the pew.

Readings should be from the pulpit Bible, if there is one, rather than from a small Bible held by the reader. The Bible that is enthroned on the pulpit or lectern, and visible to the congregation, should be used lest its integrity be undermined and it be seen merely as decoration. The pulpit Bible should therefore be the version ordinarily read in the service, and it needs to be in large, easy-to-read type. If occasionally a translation other than the pulpit Bible is used, and no pulpit edition of that translation is available, the text to be read might be typed out and placed in the pulpit Bible. Such a sheet should not be visible to the congregation.

Appropriate words for introducing the readings (112–115) and concluding them (116–118) are provided. Such words mark the reading with importance, call the people to attention, and provide an appropriate response to the reading. A brief statement can locate each reading in its larger context and make it more accessible to the hearers. Any such statement should be made after the announcement of the reading and before the call, "Hear the Word of God."

The three lessons should not be read consecutively. This taxes the congregation's attention span and compromises the unique genres of Biblical literature. Therefore this order directs that psalms, hymns, or anthems be sung between the lessons. In selecting this music, it is important to keep this section of the service carefully focused on the day's lessons. The ecumenical lectionary provides a table of psalms for use in response to the Old Testament reading. Many musical settings for these psalms are available.[33] A resource for congregational singing of the psalms is presently being developed and will appear as a part of the series of supplemental liturgical resources of which this volume is a part.

Sermon

The sermon is to be an interpretation of the Scriptures that have been read. However, the preacher need not feel compelled to expound all the interpretive possibilities of each text. The three readings appointed in the lectionary do not always relate to each other. The preacher should therefore avoid any temptation to deal substantively with all three lessons.

The sermon should normally last no longer than twenty minutes, leaving time for sacramental or nonsacramental thanksgiving. Nothing special need be prepared for the children, since the action and drama of the service, together with the frequent opportunities for participation, will engage their attention at various levels. Preaching that is sensitive to the presence of children will include illustrations that are meaningful to children.

The preacher may conclude the sermon with an ascription of praise (119–126) giving glory to God.

Response

A number of responses to the proclamation of the Word are possible. The basic response would be the singing of a hymn and the reciting of a creed or affirmation of faith (135–143). Care should be taken that affirmations of faith be widely accepted and have official ecclesiastical approval. Subjective, theologically questionable affirmations should not be imposed upon the people as creedal. Neither should affirmations be prepared for the occasion. It is the universal, catholic faith that is affirmed—the faith of the church—not a local or private expression.

If Baptism or a rite such as marriage, commissioning (confirmation), or ordination is to be celebrated, it comes at this point in the service.

An invitation to discipleship may be given. The call to conversion and discipleship must occur in some form for each generation of Christians. In the context of corporate worship, the personal decision for Christ and the affirmation of that commitment continue to be significant moments of religious encounter for many Presbyterians. Historically, the invitation has been extended by the preacher, following the sermon.

Care must be taken to ensure that the invitation is appropriate to the occasion, tasteful, mindful of the Reformed doctrine of sanctification, and not overused. Because God's kingdom advances through the *free* allegiance of its citizens, the invitation and the gestures and music that surround it must *never* be manipulative. Psychological pressure from peers, parents, and pastors is undesirable in the delicate appropriation of personal faith. Authenticity is crucial to the Spirit's free movement through this option in the liturgy.

The use of the invitation requires keen pastoral sensitivities and liturgical flexibility. An uplifted hand, an invitation to come forward, extemporaneous prayer for God's Spirit, and the laying on of hands are appropriate kinds of liturgical gestures through which the congregation may also uphold this increase in faith. Unbaptized persons responding to the invitation should be referred to preparation for Baptism and first Communion.

In using an invitation, pastors should also be aware of its natural link with the opportunity for commitment and reaffirmation provided for in the Eucharist. It is in the Eucharist, as the highest form of praise and thanksgiving, that communicants present themselves as living sacrifices, holy and acceptable to God (Rom. 12:1). This section of the liturgy properly situates personal faith within an ecclesial context. The verses from Scripture that appear as invitation to discipleship (127–134) are provided as aids for improvisation in extending an invitation.

Prayers of Intercession

Surely God's Word to us must invite our words to God. An essential part of the proclamation of the Word is our response in prayer. Prayers for others—world, nation, church, community, congregation, those in need—have found their place in Christian liturgy at this point. A variety of ways of offering these prayers is suggested in the liturgical texts included in this resource (144–166). Since these prayers are the prayers of the people, an attempt should be made to involve the people in this prayer, both in gathering concerns and in offering the prayers. These prayers need not be confined to the leadership of the minister, but may be led by a ruling elder, deacon, or lay member. Such persons should be given training in the leadership of public prayer. Concerns may be solicited from the people for inclusion in the prayers. It is appropriate for the congregation to participate by giving assent to the prayers in ways such as those suggested in the texts. If the confession of sin has been omitted, it may now be included, particularly if the Sacrament is to be celebrated. The leader of the prayers should stand near the Lord's table or close to the people.

Offering

The offering of gifts is a corporate act of self-dedication. Sentences from Scripture that underscore this may be used to introduce the offering (167–179). Music may accompany the gathering of the gifts, or the offering may be gathered in silence.

The money offering is brought forward and placed, not on the Lord's table, or on the floor, but on a side table or stand. As the gifts are brought forward, a doxological stanza (of which there are many) might be sung, with the congregation standing. Care needs to be taken lest the offering become a celebration of human generosity. Praise, not the offering, is the climax of Christian worship.

No prayer is needed, as the great prayer of thanksgiving is presently to be offered. Those bringing the offering return to their places and all sit.

C. Give Thanks to God

Preparation of the Table

The offering of monetary gifts concludes the sequence that focuses on proclamation, and it begins the thanksgiving sequence. The reason for this, as stated above, lies in the historic relation between the offering and the Eucharist whereby there was brought forward not money, but bread and wine for the Sacrament. The Genevan Reformers explicitly rejected the offering of bread and wine, although the Scottish did not.[34] The theological decision of Geneva is respected, but our Scottish history is also reflected when this order directs: "The minister(s) and elders prepare the table with bread and wine during the gathering of the gifts" (page 21). Thus while certain members of the congregation receive the offering, the minister(s) and elders bring to the Lord's table the cloths and vessels needed for the celebration.

This order prefers not to ceremonialize the preparation of the table, but to set it as simply as possible. Wine is poured into the chalice and the vessels are made ready for the serving. This can be done in silence quite eloquently. If several cups or chalices are used, it is expressive to fill them from a flagon or pitcher. Even if the people are not to drink from a common cup, one cup can be filled for use by the minister(s) and elders.

Invitation to the Lord's Table

The presiding minister gives the invitation (180–182) from the table. This should not be a homily but a genuine invitation in words of Scripture.

Although earlier Reformed rites included the words of institution at this place in the service, this order does not, preferring to use them as part of the prayer, as most other traditions do, or after the prayer as spoken commentary to the breaking of the bread and lifting of the cup. This makes it possible to use for the invitation verses containing certain other Biblical motifs that belong to the Supper, such as the Messianic banquet and the Emmaus meal from Luke, Johannine themes, a reference from Revelation, and Psalm 34. The invitation should be brief so as to facilitate the movement from preparing the table to adorning it with prayer.

The Great Prayer of Thanksgiving

Since the time of Hippolytus, the great prayer of thanksgiving (eucharistic prayer) has been introduced with a dialogue inviting the people to give thanks to God. This dialogue expresses the central emphasis of thanksgiving as well as the communal character of this action. When the people have learned these sentences, saying or singing them from memory, a festive note is imparted to the celebration.

The presiding minister stands behind the table with the elders on either side. Throughout history, the people have stood while this prayer, with its dialogue, has been said. Hippolytus' prayer even refers to this posture: ". . . giving you thanks that you have counted us worthy to stand in your presence." Standing respects the prayer's creedal and hymnic character. The people should therefore remain standing after the offering of gifts.

Throughout history, the great thanksgiving has been recognized as particularly important. Because of its liturgical centrality and its theological significance, this prayer has always been prepared with special care. It is both prayer and proclamation and should be spoken in a clear, confident voice.

The prayers contained in this volume (183–190, pages 88–118) are based upon historical tradition and ecumenical consensus. Traditionally, the body of the prayer consists of three parts and is very clearly trinitarian in its structure. A congregational acclamation may be sung or said by the people after each section.

The first part consists of praise to the first Person of the Trinity. Thanksgiving is voiced for the mighty acts of God such as creation and providence, for the sending of prophets, and for God's steadfast love. Praise for the event in salvation history being celebrated may be included. The congregational acclamation "Holy, holy, holy Lord" concludes this part. This song is the great hymn of Isaiah 6:3 and Revelation 4:8, and it also includes the song sung as Jesus rode into Jerusalem, "Hosanna! Blessed is he who comes . . ." (Matt. 21:9; Ps. 118:26).

The second part of the prayer offers praise to God for the work of Christ. Thanks is offered for Christ's ministry, his death and resurrection, and the hope of his coming. This part may be followed by a Christological acclamation such as "Christ has died. Christ is risen. Christ will come again." Other texts are available as alternatives (193–196).

The final part shifts from thanksgiving for God's mighty acts and the work of Christ to asking that the Holy Spirit be sent. Prayer is offered that the Holy Spirit may effect among us the benefits of Christ's redemption and reconciliation, empower us to faithfulness in Christ's service in the world, and lead us at last to the glory of God's kingdom.

Intercessions have been included in eucharistic prayers in both East and West since the fourth century. Prayers for the work and mission of the church flow from our thankful remembering of God's mighty acts. The great deeds of God for which we give thanks assure us that God gives strength to do God's will. In remembering, we are assured God remembers us. These intercessions may therefore be seen as an extension of the petition that the Holy Spirit may be poured out.

The prayer ends with the great "Amen" of the people. The final "Amen" has always been particularly emphasized as the congregation's completion of the opening dialogical invitation. Justin Martyr remarked, "When the prayers and eucharist are finished, all the people present give their assent with an 'Amen.' "[35]

The prayer thus encompasses the full expanse of God's creating and redeeming acts. Our praise begins with creation's dawning and ends by looking beyond time to the glory of the new age that is yet to be. The prayer is important in that in it we remember who we are, and whose we are, and where God is leading us.[36]

There is no need for the full text of the great prayer of thanksgiving to be in the hands of the people. Only the people's acclamations, with music, need be provided.

The Lord's Prayer (204–208) follows the great thanksgiving. The text should be available to the people if the contemporary translation (207) is being learned.

A fuller interpretation of the option concerning the words of institution is in order. The Reformed tradition is almost alone in isolating the Lord's words "This is my body . . . This is my blood" from the prayer over the bread and wine. How to define Christ's presence in the Eucharist was one of the major theological issues of the Reformation. The Roman Church had affirmed the power of the priest to effect an actual change in the bread and wine by properly reciting the Lord's words. It was asserted that the change occurred at the moment the words were uttered.

The Reformers felt it important to rescue Christ's presence from priestly powers, ecclesiastical discipline, and philosophical speculation. Luther redefined the nature of the change and suppressed the entire prayer, keeping only the Lord's words. Zwingli abolished the sacramental concept altogether, retaining the Supper as a memorial meal to be celebrated occasionally. Cranmer rewrote the Roman texts in English and introduced into the texts theological notes both Catholic and Protestant. Calvin and Knox spoke of the "real" though not "local" presence of Christ, and they prepared a prayer that did not include the words. Instead, the words were read as proclamation and warrant for the service before the prayer. This was done deliberately to avoid the use of the Lord's words as a kind of magic formula to convert the bread and wine into Jesus' body and blood. Separation of the "words" from the prayer also emphasized the relation between Scripture and the church's proclamation and prayer.

This order provides for the inclusion of the words of institution in some of the great thanksgiving prayers while omitting them in others. The reason for including the institution narrative in some of the prayers is to move us beyond the theological debates of the sixteenth century, since those issues are not major considerations today. Ecumenical liturgical practice is virtually universal in including the narrative in the prayer. By including the narrative in the prayer, praise to God for the gift of this Sacrament is joined to praise for all the other acts of God for which we give thanks in this prayer.

The fact that the narrative has not been included in all the prayers acknowledges that it has been the tradition for Reformed churches to exclude it from the prayer. It further reminds us that the inclusion of the words of institution is not an essential part of the prayer itself, even though the narrative is an important part of the Communion liturgy.

Since in the Reformed tradition the words of institution have been read as the Scriptural warrant for the Supper, we need to remind ourselves that when included in the prayer, the narrative is no less the warrant from Scripture than when it is read apart from the prayer. Whether made a part of the prayer or read separately, it is important that the narrative be included in each celebration of the Supper.

Breaking of the Bread

If the words of institution are not used in the great thanksgiving, they are proper for the manual acts of breaking the loaf and lifting the cup (209). If they are part of the prayer, other words are chosen (210), or the bread may be broken in silence (211), since the narrative should be used only once in the liturgy. When accompanying the manual acts, the words should be spoken slowly and in careful rhythm with the gestures. Gestures need to be expansive and smoothly paced. Nothing dare be rushed. It is important that everyone be able to see what is happening.

The use of a loaf of bread expresses the communal nature of the Sacrament, the unity of the body of Christ. A loaf makes graphic what diced bread or wafers cannot, that in partaking of the one loaf, Jesus Christ, we become one body. Paul's words are given force: "Because there is one loaf, we, many as we are, are one body; for it is one loaf of which we all partake. When we break the bread, is it not a sharing in the body of Christ?" (I Cor. 10:16–17 NEB). The loaf should not be precut, but actually broken, lest a pretense be made of the action. Use of a common cup further expresses the unity of the people in Christ.

Communion

The presiding minister may first partake and then serve those assisting, or serve them and they in turn may serve the minister. An example is thereby given to all that they may join in the feast and they are instructed how they may receive the bread and wine. This is particularly important if communicants are to be encouraged to speak words to one another at the giving of the bread and wine (214–218), or if vessels or elements are being used to which the congregation is not accustomed.

The earliest Reformed method for Communion required the people to go to the Lord's table to receive the bread and wine. "With Calvin, the people came forward as they had always done . . . one by one, receiving the bread from one Minister at one end of the table, and the Wine from another Minister at the other end."[37] In his English congregation in Geneva, John Knox had the people sit at the table, a practice that was continued by the Puritans[38] and carried to the American colonies.[39]

Pew Communion is therefore a late arrival in the Reformed tradition and is presently virtually unique to the Reformed. While it does provide an opportunity for Christians to serve one another, it nevertheless tends to reinforce the individualism and passivity that are characteristic of many sacramental occasions.

An increasing number of congregations are therefore restoring the long-standing custom of inviting the people to come to the Lord's table to receive the Sacrament. The result is that a greater sense of community and active participation is experienced. Those who are to serve are given the bread and wine at the table. They then take positions convenient to the congregation where the people may receive the elements. If a common cup is used and many are to be served, it is suggested that there be one person to serve the bread and two to administer the cup, since it takes longer to serve the cup than the bread. If desired, the option of using grape juice or wine can be provided by the two cup bearers at each station. It will quickly become apparent that people move themselves about more efficiently, easily, and informally than large, cumbersome vessels can be moved to the people.

Where a congregation is resistant to everyone drinking from the same cup, the use of a chalice with a pouring lip might be considered. Available from church supply houses, these chalices facilitate the pouring of the wine into small glasses that communicants receive as they approach the place where they will be served. The symbolism conveyed by the use of the common cup is thereby preserved, even though less forcefully.

If the congregation continues the practice of pew Communion, the bread should be in pieces large enough to be broken as it is passed. Several cups or chalices might still be used, each with a cloth for wiping the lip of the cup. The wine should immediately follow the bread, for bread and wine are not two separate courses, they are the meal. The custom of first serving the bread to everyone and then serving the wine needlessly prolongs the serving.

The custom of holding the bread or cup until all are served so that all may eat or drink in unison is discouraged. The unity of God's people is not conveyed in doing something simultaneously. The use of a single loaf and common cup more naturally and effectively expresses the communal aspects of the Sacrament.

Whether the people go to the table to receive the Sacrament or are served in the pew, there may be singing, instrumental music, or silence kept (page 25) during the serving. When all have partaken, the remaining bread and wine are quietly returned to the table.

If a prayer follows the serving, such as one of those provided in this book (219–229), it should be brief and may be prayed in unison.

Alternate Thanksgiving

If the Sacrament is not celebrated, an alternate service is outlined. It consists of substituting for the full sacramental thanksgiving a nonsacramental form that may touch many of the same emphases (197–203). This, too, springs from the proclamation and the offering of monetary gifts. When the offering is brought forward to the singing of a hymn, spiritual, or doxological stanza, the minister stands at the Lord's table and leads the same dialogue that introduces the great prayer of thanksgiving. A nonsacramental prayer of thanksgiving is then offered while all remain standing. The parallel of this prayer with the great prayer of thanksgiving is reinforced when it follows a trinitarian outline as does the sacramental prayer (see 199 and 203). The great prayers of thanksgiving (183–190) may be adapted for nonsacramental use. Those portions pertaining only to the Sacrament will of course be deleted. At the conclusion of the prayer the people respond, "Amen." The Lord's Prayer is then prayed.

This nonsacramental option indicates that the sacramental service is normative. It also maintains the emphasis of the Lord's Day service on the majesty and praise of almighty God by returning the service to its point of entry, namely, praise and thanksgiving.

After the thanksgiving (sacramental or nonsacramental), a word and sign of peace may be exchanged if not previously done.

D. Go in God's Name

The conclusion of the service should be simple and straightforward. A hymn of praise or a psalm or spiritual song is sung, the congregation standing. Brief sung acclamations or prayers are provided for Sundays when the Sacrament is celebrated. The choir moves out in procession if that is the custom. If the worship leaders process with the choir, the singing will follow the blessing.

Charge

In the words of Scripture the people are charged to be faithful as ministers in the world (230–239). If the charge follows the blessing, a ruling elder or a deacon may give the charge (preferably using 236–239), possibly standing next to the minister at the Lord's table. The charge should not be a sermonic exhortation.

Blessing

The blessing, or benediction, is said by a minister of the Word, with hands extended over the people (240–245). Hands extended over a group of people has the same meaning as the laying on of hands upon the head of one person. The blessing should be said from the Lord's table. Something as important as the blessing of God should not be spoken from behind the backs of the people.

The concluding organ music, or other instrumental music, is also a part of the service and should be heard with reverence. The people would be more likely to give it silent attention if the leaders and choir remained in their places after the dismissal. In any case, a few moments of reflection are appropriate as the people prepare to go out to serve God in the world (246–247).

This commentary has emphasized that the worship of God is the core of the Christian life. Assembled, the faithful center upon Scripture, sermon, and Sacrament. Going forth into the world, they center upon a commitment to love and justice. This community of the resurrection is sent to "make disciples of all nations, baptizing them in the name of the Father and of the Son and of the Holy Spirit" (Matt. 28:19).

At the heart of all Christian worship is the proclamation "Christ is risen!" This witness thrusts us into God's future with its promise of the new creation and the hope of redemption. The resurrection of Christ, at the heart of worship on each Lord's Day, proclaims the radical transformation of time and human behavior. "Early on the first day of the week" (Mark 16:9) the people of God gather, bringing all their cares and shattered anticipations in order to witness the resurrection anew in Word and Sacrament. Confronted with the reality of the resurrection and empowered by the Spirit, they then depart as transformed witnesses to live the new life of the kingdom, anticipating the Day of the Lord.

NOTES

1. Karl Barth, *Church Dogmatics*, ed. by G. W. Bromiley and T. F. Torrance, Vol. IV, Part 2 (Edinburgh: T. & T. Clark, 1958), p. 698.

2. "Directory for the Service of God," *The Constitution of the Presbyterian Church (U.S.A.), Part II, Book of Order 1983–85* (New York and Atlanta: Office of the General Assembly of the Presbyterian Church [U.S.A.], 1983), S-2.0400, para. 1.

3. Barth, *Church Dogmatics*, Vol. IV, Part 2, p. 709.

4. "Directory for the Service of God," S-2.0400, para. 4.

5. Ibid., S-1000.

6. Ibid., S-1.000, para. 5.

7. John Calvin, *Institutes of the Christian Religion*, tr. by Henry Beveridge (Wm. B. Eerdmans Publishing Co., 1953), Vol. II, p. 601.

8. *Calvin: Theological Treatises*, tr. and ed. by J. K. S. Reid, The Library of Christian Classics (Westminster Press, 1954), p. 66.

9. "Directory for the Service of God," S-3.0500 (a).

10. "Directory for the Service of God," S-2.0500.

11. Ibid., para. 4.

12. Ibid., para. 4.

13. Ibid., S-2.0400, para. 4.

14. *Reformed Liturgy and Music*, Vol. VIII, No. 5 (Fall 1974); reprinted in *Let Us Worship God!* (Louisville, Ky.: Joint Office of Worship, 1980).

15. See Task Force on Language About God, Advisory Council on Discipleship and Worship, *Language About God—Opening the Door* (New York: The United Presbyterian Church in the U.S.A., 1975); Task Force on Language About God, Advisory Council on Discipleship and Worship, *The Power of Language Among the People of God* (New York: The United Presbyterian Church in the U.S.A., 1979). These are available in one booklet from The Advisory Council on Discipleship and Worship, 1020 Interchurch Center, 475 Riverside Drive, New York, NY 10115. Also see "Language About God," *Minutes of the 120th General Assembly, Presbyterian Church in the United States, Part I, Journal* (Atlanta: Stated Clerk of the General Assembly of the Presbyterian Church in the United States, 1980), pp. 164–173.

16. Peter G. Cobb, "The Liturgy of the Word in the Early Church," in *The Study of the Liturgy*, ed. by Cheslyn Jones, Geoffrey Wainwright, and Edward Yarnold, S.J. (New York: Oxford University Press, 1978), p. 182.

17. William D. Maxwell, *The Liturgical Portions of the Genevan Service Book* (London: Faith Press, 1965), p. 70.

18. James Hastings Nichols, *Corporate Worship in the Reformed Tradition* (Westminster Press, 1968), p. 98.

19. Ibid.

20. "The Confession of 1967," *The Constitution of The United Presbyterian Church in the United States of America, Part I, Book of Confessions* (New York: Office of the General Assembly of The United Presbyterian Church in the United States of America, 1967), 9.27.

21. J. G. Davies, ed., *A Dictionary of Liturgy and Worship* (Macmillan Co., 1972), p. 211.

22. The Presbyterian version of the ecumenical lectionary is found in *The Worshipbook* (Westminster Press, 1970, 1972), pp. 167–175. A full discussion of the purpose and use of a lectionary is found in Horace T. Allen, Jr., *A Handbook for the Lectionary* (Geneva Press, 1980). A recently completed revision of the lectionary prepared by an ecumenical committee whose task was to resolve the differences between the versions of the lectionary is now incorporated into *The Presbyterian Planning Calendar*. The complete lectionary, entitled *The Common Lectionary*, may be purchased from the Church Hymnal Corporation (800 Second Avenue, New York, NY 10017). Each issue of *Reformed Liturgy and Music* beginning with the Summer 1983 issue (and to continue through the Spring 1986 issue) includes helps for using the newly revised lectionary.

23. Dietrich Bonhoeffer, *Psalms: The Prayer Book of the Bible*, tr. by James H. Burtness (Augsburg Publishing House, 1970), p. 15.

24. Harold M. Daniels, *A Commentary on the Service for the Lord's Day* (Geneva Press, 1981), p. 21.

25. "The Heidelberg Catechism," *The Constitution of The United Presbyterian Church in the United States of America, Part I, Book of Confessions*, 4.116.

26. A second-century witness, Justin, testified in his *Apologia:* "It is on Sunday that we all assemble, because Sunday is the first day: the day on which God transformed darkness and matter and created the world, and the day on which Jesus Christ our Savior rose from the dead. He was crucified on the eve of Saturn's day, and on the day after, that is, on the day of the sun, he appeared to his apostles and disciples and taught them what we have now offered for your examination" (Lucien Deiss, C.S.Sp. [ed.], *Springtime of the Liturgy*, tr. by Matthew J. O'Connell [Liturgical Press, 1979], p. 94).

27. See Oscar Cullmann, "The Meaning of the Lord's Supper in Primitive Christianity" in Oscar Cullmann and F. J. Leenhardt, *Essays on the Lord's Supper*, tr. by J. G. Davies (John Knox Press, 1958), pp. 5–23.

28. To avoid sexually exclusive language, some editing may be necessary. The following service books have editions of the Psalter that should be helpful: The Episcopal Church, *The Book of Common Prayer* (New York: The Church Hymnal Corporation and Seabury Press, 1977); Lutheran Church in America (and other Lutheran Churches), *Lutheran Book of Worship* (Min-

neapolis: Augsburg Publishing House; Philadelphia: Board of Publication, Lutheran Church in America, 1978).

29. "In the early Church it was a widespread principle that on Sundays and during the joyful Easter season (hence, during the seven weeks between Easter and Pentecost) no penance could be performed. During this time, as we read in Tertullian, one should not fast, nor should one pray kneeling, as the penitents had to do" (Josef A. Jungmann, *The Early Liturgy*, tr. by Francis A. Brunner [University of Notre Dame Press, 1959], p. 245).

30. In Calvin's Strassburg Order the rubric and text are as follows: "*Now the Minister delivers some word of Scripture to console the conscience; and then he pronounces the absolution in this manner:*

"Let each of you truly acknowledge that he is a sinner, humbling himself before God, and believe that the heavenly Father wills to be gracious unto him in Jesus Christ.

"To all those that repent in this wise, and look to Jesus Christ for their salvation, I declare that the absolution of sins is effected, in the name of the Father, and of the Son, and of the Holy Spirit. Amen." Bard Thompson, ed., *Liturgies of the Western Church* (World Publishing Co., 1961), p. 198.

In the *Institutes* Calvin gave stress to the declaration of pardon: "For when the whole church stands, as it were, before God's judgment seat, confesses itself guilty, and has its sole refuge in God's mercy, it is no common or light solace to have present there the ambassador of Christ, armed with the mandate of reconciliation, by whom it hears proclaimed its absolution" (*Calvin: Institutes of the Christian Religion*, ed. by John T. McNeill, tr. by Ford Lewis Battles, The Library of Christian Classics [Westminster Press, 1960], III. iv. 14).

31. John Calvin, *Institutes of the Christian Religion*, tr. by Henry Beveridge, Vol. I, p. 71.

32. Prayers for the day will be found in *The Worshipbook*, pp. 135–163. Allen, *A Handbook for the Lectionary*, contains others.

33. Suggestions for singing the psalms are a regular feature in the lectionary helps in *Reformed Liturgy and Music*. Specific recommendations are given for musical settings to be sung by the congregation.

34. W. D. Maxwell sums up sixteenth-century practice this way: "The practice at Strassburg from the beginning of the Reformation was to bring the Bread and Wine to the Holy Table (in all likelihood from a side Altar) immediately following the singing of the Creed after the Sermon. . . . In this, they simply prepared the Elements at the same point in the service as had been done in the Mass.

"Calvin carried on the same custom, as we see by his rubric of 1545: '*Cependant le Ministre prépare le pain et le vin sur la table*,' save that he made the preparation while the people sang the Creed. . . .

"It is altogether probable that in [Knox's] *Forme of Prayers* (1556) the same custom was followed; had it been different, it is almost certain that the rubric would have been explicit to that effect. There is one slight difference, however, namely, that this 'furnishing' of the Table was not done in the English Congregation during the recitation of the Creed, but during the singing of a Psalm immediately following the Creed before the Exhortation. . . .

"Reformed Scottish practice was slightly different to this, and the difference in the first instance was very likely a result of the shortage of Ministers. In Scotland, it seems, the Deacons (this time in the Reformed sense of the word) early were delegated by the Minister to the task of bringing in the Elements from the Vestry to the Holy Table during the singing of the Psalm following the Creed. . . . Elders also were sometimes invited to serve in this capacity. In the early Scottish tradition the Tables were never 'furnished' before the service began" (Maxwell, *The Liturgical Portions of the Genevan Service Book*, pp. 132–134).

35. Deiss, *Springtime of the Liturgy*, p. 92.

36. For more on the great prayer of thanksgiving, as well as eucharistic theology and practice, see Arlo D. Duba, "The Lord's Supper," in Daniel B. Wessler, Cynthia A. Jarvis, Harold M. Daniels, Arlo D. Duba, and Melva W. Costen, *Worship in the Community of Faith* (Louisville, Ky.: Joint Office of Worship, 1982), pp. 98–141.

37. Maxwell, *The Liturgical Portions of the Genevan Service Book*, pp. 137–138. See also Nichols, *Corporate Worship in the Reformed Tradition*, pp. 49–50.

38. Maxwell, op. cit.

39. Julius Melton, *Presbyterian Worship in America* (John Knox Press, 1967), p. 26.

SOURCES OF THE LITURGICAL TEXTS

This volume contains a rich blend of prayers both from our liturgical heritage and from contemporary sources. New prayers, prepared for this book, are also included. To enable users to appreciate the breadth of this resource, sources are identified. These abbreviations are used in the source notes.

ALT	*At the Lord's Table.* United Methodist, 1981.
APB	*An Australian Prayer Book.* The Church of England in Australia, 1978.
ASB	*The Alternate Service Book 1980.* Church of England.
BCO (1874)	*The Book of Common Order.* Church Service Society, Scotland, 1874.
BCO (1940)	*The Book of Common Order.* Church of Scotland, 1940.
BCP (1549)	*The Book of Common Prayer.* Church of England, 1549.
BCP (1662)	*The Book of Common Prayer.* Church of England, 1662.
BCP (1928)	*The Book of Common Prayer.* Episcopal Church, U.S.A., 1928.
BCP	*The Book of Common Prayer.* Episcopal Church, U.S.A., 1977.
BCW (1906)	*The Book of Common Worship.* Presbyterian, U.S.A., 1906.
BCW (1932)	*The Book of Common Worship.* Presbyterian, U.S.A., 1932.
BCW (1946)	*The Book of Common Worship.* Presbyterian, U.S.A., 1946.
BCWP	*The Book of Common Worship: Provisional Services.* Presbyterian, U.S.A., 1966.
COCU	*An Order of Worship.* Consultation on Church Union, 1968.
CPA	*A Chain of Prayer Across the Ages.* Comp. by Selina F. Fox, 6th ed., 1941.
GS	*General Services.* United Methodist Church, 1984.
ICET	International Consultation on English Texts.
LBW	*Lutheran Book of Worship.* Lutheran, U.S.A., 1978.
PBCP	*Presbyterian Book of Common Prayer.* Ed. by Charles W. Shields, U.S.A., 1864.
RS	*The Sacramentary.* Roman Catholic, 1974.
SBCP (1637)	Scottish *Book of Common Prayer,* 1637.
SLD	*Service for the Lord's Day and Lectionary for the Christian Year.* Presbyterian, U.S.A., 1964.

UCA	*Uniting Church Worship Services: Holy Communion.* The Uniting Church in Australia, 1980.
UCC	*Service Book.* United Church of Canada, 1969.
URC	*A Book of Services.* United Reformed Church in England and Wales, 1980.
WBK	*The Worshipbook—Services and Hymns.* Presbyterian, U.S.A., 1972.
WGT	*We Gather Together.* United Methodist, 1980.

Abbreviations for Bible translations are:

KJV	*King James Version*
NEB	*The New English Bible*
RSV	*Revised Standard Version*
TEV	*Today's English Version (Good News Bible)*

1. WBK. Altered.
2. BCW (1946), BCO (1940). Altered.
3. BCW (1946), BPC (1928), BCP. Altered. Derives from William Bright's *Ancient Collects.* Zech. 12:10; John 4:23.
4. BCW (1946), WBK. Altered.
5. *The Book of Common Prayer* of St. Giles Cathedral. Altered.
6. BCW (1906, 1932, 1946), SLD, BCP (1549), PBCP, BCP. Altered. Based on Eph. 2:20–22 and 4:3.
7. BCW (1946). Altered.
8. CPA. Altered. Attributed to Augustine, although source is doubtful.
9. LBW.
10. LBW.
11. BCO (1979). BCP (1549 and each succeeding edition). Altered.
12. BCW (1946). Altered.
13. WBK.
14. SLD, BCWP. Altered.
15. WBK. Altered.
16. WBK. Altered.
17. WBK.
18. Ex. 20:1–17 RSV; Matt. 22:37–40 RSV. Altered.
19. An ancient salutation based on the greeting of Boaz and the response of the reapers (Ruth 2:4).
20. II Thess. 3:18 RSV. Cf. Rom. 16:20; I Cor. 16:23; II Cor. 13:14; Gal. 6:18; Phil. 4:13; I Thess. 5:18; Philemon 25; Rev. 22:21.
21. II Cor. 13:14 RSV. Altered.
22. Rom. 1:7; I Cor. 1:3; II Cor. 1:2; Eph. 1:2; Phil. 1:2; Philemon 3. RSV. Cf. Gal. 1:3; Col. 1:2; I Thess. 1:1; II Thess. 1:2.
23. I Tim. 1:2; II Tim. 1:2 RSV. Cf. II John 3.
24. II Peter 1:2 NEB.
25. Rev. 1:4, 5 RSV. Altered.
26. SBCP (1637).
27. Based on Luke 24:34.

28. Ps. 124:8 RSV.
29. I Cor. 5:7, 8 KJV.
30. Ps. 116:12, 13 RSV. Altered.
31. Ps. 34:8 RSV. Altered.
32. Ps. 118:24 RSV. Altered.
33. Ps. 34:3 RSV. Altered.
34. Ps. 106:1 RSV. Altered. See also I Chron. 16:34, 41; II Chron. 5:13; 7:3, 6; 20:21; Ezra 3:11; Ps. 107:1; 118:1, 2, 3, 4; 136:1, 2, 3, etc.; 138:8; Jer. 33:11.
35. Based on RSV, TEV, and NEB translations of Ps. 95:1, 2.
36. Based on RSV, TEV, and NEB translations of Ps. 24:1.
37. Isa. 40:31 RSV. Altered.
38. Ps. 100:1, 2 RSV. Altered.
39. Ps. 47:1 RSV. Altered.
40. I Peter 1:3 RSV. Altered.
41. Matt. 28:19 RSV.
42. John 1:1 RSV.
43. Rom. 5:5 RSV.
44. Isa. 57:15. Based on NEB and TEV.
45. Ps. 46:1–3 RSV. Altered.
46. John 4:24 RSV. Altered.
47. Rom. 12:1 RSV. Altered.
48. John 3:17 RSV.
49. I John 4:7, 8 RSV. Altered.
50. Mal. 1:11 RSV. Altered.
51. Rev. 4:8 TEV. Altered.
52. BCW (1906, 1932, 1946). Appears in eleventh-century missals and the Sarum missal. BCP (1549, 1552, etc.), BCP, BCO (1940, 1979), LBW. Version here is that of LBW.
53. Based on a prayer written by James F. White and Susan J. White.
54. BCW (1946), BCO (1940). Altered.
55. BCW (1906, 1932, 1946), BCO (1940). Adapted by Henry van Dyke for BCW. Altered.
56. BCW (1906, 1932), BCO (1874). Derives from Gelasian Sacramentary. Altered.
57. Based on a prayer from BCO (1979).
58–62. Written for this resource.
63. Based on litanies from the Eastern liturgies of St. Basil and St. John Chrysostom. LBW. Altered.
64. I John 1:8, 9 RSV. Altered. BCWP. Cf. WBK.
65. Based on Rom. 5:8 NEB, and Heb. 4:16 RSV. WBK.
66. Heb. 4:14, 16 RSV. Altered.
67. I John 2:1, 2 NEB. Altered.
68. Matt. 11:28–30 RSV. Altered.
69. Ps. 34:18 RSV. Altered.
70. John 3:16, 17 RSV. Altered.
71. Heb. 10:22 RSV. Altered.
72. Isa. 30:18. Based on RSV and NEB.
73. Jer. 31:33, 34 RSV. Altered.
74. BCW (1946). Revised. Uses BCP revision.

75. BCWP. Altered.
76. WGT. Altered.
77. BCW (1906, 1932, 1946). Abbreviation by Henry van Dyke for BCW. Revised.
78. WBK. Altered.
79. BCW (1932, 1946), BCP (1552–1928), BCP, BCO (1874). Based on Rom. 7:8–25. Other Scriptural allusions: Isa. 53:6; Ps. 119:176; I Peter 2:25; Ps. 51:13; Rom. 15:8; I John 2:12; Titus 2:11, 12; John 14:13. Revised.
80. WBK. Altered.
81. BCW (1946). Ps. 51:1, 10–12; Micah 6:8. Revised.
82. BCW (1906, 1932, 1946), SLD, BCWP, BCO (1940), COCU (in part). Altered by Henry van Dyke for BCW. Revised.
83. BCW (1946). Agreed liturgical text prepared by ICET. BCO (1979).
84. Agreed liturgical text prepared by ICET. BCO (1979).
85. SLD, BCWP, BCO (1979).
86. Greek text of "Lord, have mercy."
87–88. Based on declarations of pardon contained in BCW (1906, 1932, 1946). Revised.
89. WBK. I Tim. 1:15 RSV; I Peter 2:24. Based on RSV and Phillips translation.
90. WBK. Rom. 8:34 Phillips translation; II Cor. 5:17 Phillips translation. Altered.
91. Rom. 6:8, 11 RSV.
92. BCW (1906, 1932, 1946), BCO (1979). Agreed liturgical text prepared by ICET.
93. Trisagion from Eastern liturgy, which came to be used in Gallican liturgies of the West. Although included in early editions of the BCP, it is included in the current BCP as an alternate to the "Lord, have mercy" for the first time. In Eastern practice it is repeated three times.
94. WBK.
95. LBW. Based on Rev. 5:12, 9, 13; 7:10, 12; 19:4, 6–9.
96. Ps. 103:8, 10–12. LBW and BCP Psalter. Altered.
97. Ps. 145:8, 9, 18, 19. LBW and BCP Psalter. Altered.
98. Cf. Col. 3:13. John 20:19, 21, 26 RSV. Cf. Col. 3:15 and III John 15.
99. Col. 3:15. Based on RSV and NEB. John 20:19, 21, 26 RSV. Cf. Col. 3:15 and III John 15.
100. Written for this resource. John 20:19, 21, 26 RSV. Cf. Col. 3:15 and III John 3:15.
101. UCC.
102. WBK. Altered.
103. WBK. Altered.
104. WGT.
105. Source unknown. Altered. Matt. 4:4 and Deut. 8:3.
106. Source unknown. Altered.
107. BCO (1940), UCA. Revised. Ps. 119:105.
108. BCO (1940). Ancient collect, source unknown. James 1:17; Eph. 1:17; II Peter 1:3. Revised.
109. BCO (1940). Col. 2:3; Ps. 119:18. Revised.

110. Source unknown.
111. BCP. Altered. Based on Rom. 15:4. Composed for BCP (1549).
113. BCW (1946), SLD, LBW, BCP, RS. Revised in accordance with LBW.
116. BCP.
117. RS.
118. BCW (1946), SLD, LBW, BCP, RS. Revised in accordance with LBW.
119. Rev. 7:12 NEB. BCW (1946), BCWP, WBK.
120. I Tim. 1:17. Based on NEB. BCW (1946), WBK.
121. Eph. 3:20 RSV. BCW (1932, 1946), BCWP.
122. Rev. 5:12 RSV.
123. Rev. 1:5, 6 RSV. Altered.
124. I Tim. 6:15, 16 RSV. Altered.
125. Rom. 11:33, 36 RSV. Altered.
126. Based on I Peter 5:10, 11.
127. Isa. 55:1, 2 RSV. Altered.
128. Acts 2:38, 39 RSV. Altered.
129. Mark 1:16, 17 RSV. Altered.
130. Matt. 11:28–30 RSV. Altered.
131. Isa. 1:16–18 RSV. Altered.
132. Rom. 12:1, 2 RSV. Altered.
133. Acts 16:30, 31 RSV. Altered.
134. Rev. 3:20 RSV. Altered.
135. Agreed liturgical text prepared by ICET. The text has been altered in two places. ICET text reads: "For us men and for our salvation." The word "men" has been deleted. This does not change the meaning and is faithful to the original in the light of today's English usage. ICET text reads: "and was made man." The text in this resource reads: "and was made human." These changes in the ICET text were incorporated following ecumenical discussions and agreements.
136. Agreed liturgical text prepared by ICET.
137. Rom. 8:35, 37–39 RSV. Altered.
138. Rom. 8:1, 28, 38, 39 RSV. Altered.
139. WBK. Based on I Cor. 15:1–6; Mark 16:9 (16:1–9); Matt. 16:16; Rev. 22:13; John 20:28.
140. Col. 1:15–20 RSV. Altered.
141. Phil. 2:5b–11 RSV. Altered.
142. I Cor. 12:3; Rom. 10:9 RSV.
143. Matt. 16:16 RSV. Altered.
144. Adapted from WBK. The prayer "Almighty God, in Jesus Christ . . ." is from SLD and BCWP and is altered. The prayer "Creator God, you made . . ." is a revision of a prayer from the WBK. The prayer "Gracious God, you have called . . ." is also a revision of a prayer from the WBK.
145. Adapted from a litany in BCP that is based on litanies from the Eastern liturgies of St. Basil and St. John Chrysostom. The LBW also has a version of this ancient litany with musical settings. See liturgical text 63 in this resource, where an abbreviated form is used as an opening litany.
146. Adapted from BCP.
147. Adapted from BCP. The first two petitions derive from England, the third and fourth are from Africa.

148. The prayer "O God, our help . . ." is a revision of a prayer from the WBK. The prayer "God of compassion, in Jesus Christ . " was written for this resource. The prayer "Eternal God . . ." is a revision of a prayer from the WBK. The prayer "God of compassion, we remember . . ." is a revision of the prayer of the Industrial Christian Fellowship (England) and is included in the BCP and LBW. The revision included in this resource is altered from the LBW version.

149. Based on BCW (1946).

150. WBK. Altered.

151. UCC. Altered.

152. Prayer based on three prayers in BCW (1946). Includes allusions to II Tim. 4:7 and I Cor. 2:9.

153. LBW. Altered.

154. LBW. Altered.

155. BCP. Altered.

156. BCP. Altered. This collect dates from the eighth century and derives from the Eastern Orthodox liturgies of St. Basil and St. John Chrysostom.

157. WBK.

158. WBK.

159. WBK. Altered.

160. LBW. Altered.

161. BCP. Altered. Biblical allusions include: Acts 17:26; Eph. 2:17; Isa. 57:19; Joel 2:28; and Acts 2:17.

162. BCP.

163. BCW (1906, 1932, 1946), SLD, BCWP, PBCP, BCP (1544–1979). From the Eastern Orthodox liturgies of St. John Chrysostom and St. Basil. Includes Biblical allusion to Matt. 18:20.

164. First part of prayer from ASB.

165. ASB. Altered.

166. BCP (1549–1979). COCU. Altered.

167. BCP. Altered.

168. Eph. 5:2 RSV.

169. Ps. 24:1. Based on NEB and TEV.

170. Matt. 6:19–21 RSV.

171. Matt. 10:8b KJV. Altered.

172. Rom. 12:6–8 RSV. Altered.

173. II Cor. 8:9 RSV. Altered.

174. II Cor. 9:6 RSV. Altered.

175. II Cor. 9:7 RSV. Altered.

176. Gal. 6:2 RSV.

177. Heb. 13:16 RSV. Altered.

178. Rev. 4:11 NEB. Altered.

179. I Chron. 29:11 RSV. Altered.

180. WBK. Altered. Biblical quotations from Luke 12:29 and Luke 24:30–31.

181. BCW (1946). Matt. 11:28–29 and John 6:35, 37 RSV, altered; Matt. 5:6 RSV, altered.

182. Rev. 3:20 RSV, altered; Ps. 34:8, altered.

183. WBK. Revised. The opening dialogue and "Holy, holy, holy Lord" are agreed liturgical texts prepared by ICET with one slight alteration in the dialogue. In the last line of the dialogue the ICET text reads: "give him

thanks." The text in this resource reads: "give our thanks." The memorial acclamation "Christ has died . . ." is taken from the RS and has wide ecumenical usage. The variation for Trinity Sunday is adapted from RS and LBW, and the variation for Christ the King is adapted from RS. Some of the Biblical allusions in the seasonal variations are as follows: Advent—Amos 5:24; Nativity of Jesus Christ/Christmas—John 1:14; Phil. 2:9; Baptism of the Lord—Luke 4:18–19; Passion Sunday/Palm Sunday—John 12:32; Ascension of the Lord—Phil. 2:9–10; All Saints' Day—Heb. 12:1; I Peter 5:4; Baptism—Rom. 6:4; Christian Marriage I—Eph. 5:26–27; Rev. 19:8–9; Christian Burial—Rom. 8:38, 39.

184. Written for this resource. The opening dialogue, the "Holy, holy, holy Lord," and the memorial acclamation are as stated in note 183 above. In keeping with the tradition of including intercessions in the eucharistic prayer, great thanksgivings B (184) and E (187) provide intercessions for optional use.

185. BCW (1946). Revised. The prayer included in BCW (1946) is a revision of the eucharistic prayer in BCW (1932) and BCW (1906). The BCW prayer is an alteration of BCP (1661) and PBCP. The opening dialogue and "Holy, holy, holy Lord" are as stated in note 183. The memorial acclamation has been added and is as stated in note 183. The words of institution have also been added for optional use.

186. A translation of the ancient eucharistic prayer of Hippolytus of Rome, dating from about 215. It is the earliest-known text for this prayer, and it therefore has great ecumenical significance. The text is based on a translation made by the International Commission on English in the Liturgy. The opening dialogue is as stated in note 183. The "Holy, holy, holy Lord" is not included in this prayer, for it was not a part of the original prayer.

187. This prayer is the work of a group of American Catholic, Anglican, and Protestant scholars who in 1974 gathered to draft a prayer that the major American churches might approve. To this end they adapted the Alexandrine Liturgy of St. Basil (fourth century). The Liturgy of St. Basil was particularly suited, not only because it has ancient roots but because it has appeal in both Eastern and Western traditions and possesses a breadth of scope. Episcopalians have included it in the BCP; the Consultation on Church Union included it in *Word Bread Cup;* and the Methodists have included it in their supplemental worship resource ALT. The Inter-Lutheran Commission on Worship has authorized its use. A comparable prayer is included in the RS. The opening dialogue and "Holy, holy, holy Lord" are as stated in note 183.

188. This prayer was developed by the Commission on Worship of the Consultation on Church Union and appears in its publication *The Sacrament of the Lord's Supper: A New Text 1984*. The opening dialogue, the "Holy, holy, holy Lord," and the memorial acclamation are as stated in note 183.

189. This prayer is based on John Calvin's exhortation (1542) and other of Calvin's writings. Although Calvin provided prayers for use in celebrating the Lord's Supper, none of them correspond directly with the traditional eucharistic prayer. This prayer borrows from his long exhortation that followed the recital of the words of institution. The opening dialogue and "Holy, holy, holy Lord" (both as stated in note 183) and the memorial acclamation from the RS, which are included in this prayer, were not part of the Genevan liturgy.

190. This prayer was written for this resource.

191. Agreed liturgical text prepared by ICET. Isa. 6:1–3; Rev. 4:8; Ps. 118:26; Matt. 21:9. This is a traditional part of classic eucharistic prayers and has been included in virtually all but the earliest eucharistic prayers.

192. The agreed liturgical text prepared by ICET that appears as 191, but omitting the *Benedictus qui venit* (Ps. 118:26; Matt. 21:9).

193. RS.

194. BCP. This acclamation is the one that appears most frequently in Eastern liturgies, where the people have been more active participants than in the Western liturgies.

195. RS.

196. RS.

197. The agreed text for the dialogue of eucharistic prayers prepared by ICET.

198. An abbreviated form of 197.

199. UCC.

200. WBK. Altered.

201. BCW (1906, 1932, 1946). Louis F. Benson. Revised. James 1:17.

202. BCW (1906, 1932, 1946), PBCP, BCP (1662–1928), BCP, BCO (1874, 1940). Appearing in the BCP (1661), it was an alteration of a prayer by Bishop Reynolds. Altered.

203. Written for this resource. This is an adaptation of 190, for nonsacramental use.

204. BCP.

205. ALT.

206. Written for this resource.

207. Agreed text prepared by ICET.

208. BCW (1906, 1932, 1946).

209. Based on I Cor. 11:23–26 and Luke 22:19–20 RSV. BCW (1906, 1932, 1946), SLD, BCWP, WBK.

210. I Cor. 10:17, 16b, 16a NEB. Altered. The last line is from BCP and derives from fourth-century Eastern liturgies: "The holy for the holy," or "Holy things for holy people."

211. BCP. Derives from fourth-century Eastern liturgies: "The holy for the holy," or "Holy things for holy people."

212. Agreed text prepared by ICET.

213. Alternate agreed text prepared by ICET.

214. A variation of 216.

215. COCU. A variation of 216.

216. BCP.

217. LBW.

218. A variation of 216.

219. WBK. Ps. 103:1, 2 RSV. Altered.

220. URC. Altered.

221. GS.

222. RS. Altered.

223. SLD. This prayer was used by the Westminster divines in 1647 Revised.

224. RS. Altered.

225. UCA. Altered.
226. APB, UCA. Altered.
227. BCP. Altered.
228. WGT. Altered.
229. Agreed text of ICET. Luke 2:29–32.
230. WBK. Altered. From proposed BCP (1928). Formed of a composite ot Scriptures: II Tim. 2:1; Eph. 6:10; I Thess. 5:21; and Acts 2:46.
231. I Cor. 16:13, 14 RSV. Altered.
232. Col. 3:17 RSV. Altered.
233. Micah 6:8 RSV. Altered.
234. I John 3:23 NEB. Altered.
235. Matt. 22:37–40 NEB. Altered.
236. BCP.
237. APB, UCA. Altered.
238. BCP.
239. BCP.
240. BCW (1906, 1932, 1946), WBK. I Cor. 13:14 RSV. Altered.
241. BCW (1906, 1932, 1946). Num. 6:24. Based on RSV and TEV. This blessing was included in John Calvin's liturgy, 1542.
242. BCW (1906, 1932, 1946), BCP (198), BCO (1940, 1979). Phil. 4:7.
243. BCW (1946). I Thess. 5:23 RSV. Altered.
244. Rom. 15:13 RSV. Altered.
245. BCW (1906, 1932, 1946), SLD, BCWP. Heb. 13:20, 21 RSV. Altered.
246. BCP, LBW. Altered.
247. LBW.

FOR FURTHER READING

The following is a brief bibliography to provide those who use this resource with further historical, theological, and practical information and help in understanding and implementing the Service for the Lord's Day contained in this volume.

Allen, Horace T., Jr. *A Handbook for the Lectionary*. Geneva Press, 1980.

The first section of this book, "Understanding the Lectionary," is an excellent introduction to the use of a lectionary. It draws from history and theology in making practical suggestions. The section "Using the Lectionary" now has limited value for those using the new consensus lectionary, which is incorporated into *The Presbyterian Planning Calendar* (see above, page 174, note 22). Helps comparable to those included in this section, correlated with the new consensus lectionary, are now a regular feature of each issue of *Reformed Liturgy and Music* (see below). (CS/MDS)

Burkhart, John E. *Worship*. Westminster Press, 1982.

Burkhart, a McCormick Seminary professor, draws upon Biblical studies and social anthropology in this engagingly written theology of worship. (CSC)

Consultation on Church Union. *Word Bread Cup*. Cincinnati: Forward Movement Publications, 1978.

A brief booklet that describes the service of proclamation and the Lord's Supper, and provides guidelines for planning the service. Four eucharistic prayers are included together with the agreed liturgical texts of the International Consultation on English Texts. Order from Forward Movement Publications, 412 Sycamore Street, Cincinnati, OH 45202.

Daniels, Harold M. *A Commentary on The Service for the Lord's Day*. Geneva Press, 1981.

Written to help lay people understand the meaning of the order and actions of the Service for the Lord's Day included in *The Worshipbook,* this booklet comments on each portion of the service. (CS/MDS)

________, ed. *Worship in the Community of Faith*. Louisville, Ky.: Joint Office of Worship, 1982.

Essays on the theology and practice of worship by five Presbyterian leaders in the field of worship are contained in this highly useful resource for study by pastors, sessions, worship committees, and adult groups. It includes sections on Biblical and Reformed worship (Daniel B. Wessler); reading and interpreting Scripture (Cynthia A. Jarvis); Baptism (Harold M. Daniels); the Lord's Supper (Arlo D. Duba); and Sacraments in life (Melva W. Costen). Reflection and action suggestions are included to facilitate group study. (JOW)

Davies, J. G., ed. *The Westminster Dictionary of Worship*. Westminster Press, 1979.

A reissue of *A Dictionary of Liturgy and Worship* published by Macmillan in 1972, this volume is a highly useful source of information on the history and practice of worship. (CSC)

Hoon, Paul W. *The Integrity of Worship*. Abingdon Press, 1971.

A careful, balanced Protestant theology of worship. (CSC)

Jones, Cheslyn; Wainwright, Geoffrey; and Yarnold, Edward, S.J., eds. *The Study of Liturgy*. New York: Oxford University Press, 1978.

A comprehensive treatment of many aspects of liturgy from the major Christian traditions, addressing historical and contemporary pastoral concerns. (CSC)

Kirk, James G. *When We Gather: A Book of Prayers for Worship*. Geneva Press, 1983.

A collection of prayers for each Sunday of the year based on the lessons in *The Common Lectionary* (see page 174, note 22). A volume is projected for each of the three cycles of the lectionary. (CSC)

Lawrence, Joy E., and Ferguson, John A. *A Musician's Guide to Church Music*. Pilgrim Press, 1981.

A comprehensive and practical handbook for church musicians. Useful. (CSC)

Nichols, James Hastings. *Corporate Worship in the Reformed Tradition*. Westminster Press, 1968.

Unfortunately out of print, this book surveys Reformed liturgical history. It is important for knowledge of the roots of Presbyterian worship. Look for it in church libraries.

Reformed Liturgy and Music.

A quarterly journal of the Joint Office of Worship, on worship and music from the perspective of the Reformed tradition. It regularly includes articles on a variety of subjects by leaders in the field of worship. Regular columns, book reviews, and music reviews keep readers current in resources and events and provide guidance to pastors, musicians, and worship committees. The journal regularly provides information about the development of the series of supplemental liturgical resources of which this volume is the first. Articles on the subject of each supplemental resource are planned in relation to the publication of each resource. The Fall 1984 and Winter 1985 issues will be particularly useful in relation to *The Service for the Lord's Day.* (JOW)

Reformed Liturgy and Music, Vol. XVI, No. 1 (Winter 1982).

This special issue on the Lord's Supper contains the following articles: "A Theology of the Lord's Supper from the Perspective of the Reformed Tradition" (Robert M. Shelton); "Reclaiming the Unity of Word and Sacrament in Presbyterian and Reformed Worship" (Thomas G. Long); "Function and Form of the Eucharistic Prayer" (James F. White); "Singing the Liturgy: Music for the Lord's Supper" (Marilyn Keiser); "Offering and Collection in the Reformed Tradition" (Arlo D. Duba); "A Sketchbook: Preaching and Worship" (David G. Buttrick). (JOW)

Reformed Liturgy and Music, Vol. XVII, No. 1 (Winter 1983).

This special issue on preaching contains the following articles: "Musings of a Homiletics Professor" (Robert M. Shelton); "Theology of the Word" (Ronald E. Sleeth); "Trends in Preaching" (Thomas G. Long); "On Preaching a Parable: The Problem of Homiletic Method" (David G. Buttrick); "Music, Rhetoric, and Preaching" (William J. Carl III); "After the Divorce—the Sermon at Home in the Liturgy" (David H. C. Read); "Sermons and Planning Music" (Charles Huddleston Heaton); "Minister of the Word?" (Fred R. Anderson). (JOW)

Thompson, Bard, ed. *Liturgies of the Western Church.* World Publishing Company, Meridian Books, 1961.

A collection of the major Western liturgies with historical notes. (CSC)

White, James F. *Introduction to Christian Worship.* Abingdon Press, 1980.

White, an important writer in liturgical studies, provides a basic introduction dealing with the most important aspects of worship. Ecumenical in perspective, it is packed with information. (CSC)

________. *Sacraments as God's Self Giving.* Abingdon Press, 1983.

The latest book to come from James White, this is a highly readable survey of contemporary sacramental theology. Ecumenical. (CSC)

Willimon, William H. *Word, Water, Wine, and Bread: How Worship Has Changed Over the Years.* Judson Press, 1980.

A brief introductory history of worship. Willimon writes from the conviction that worship is central to the life and mission of the church, and that liturgical reform has to do with the renewal of the church.

(CS) Curriculum Services, P.O. Box 868, William Penn Annex, Philadelphia, PA 19105.

(CSC) Cokesbury Service Centers

1661 North Northwest Highway, Park Ridge, IL 60068
312/299-4411

1635 Adrian Road, Burlingame, CA 94010
415/692-3562

201 Eighth Avenue, South, P.O. Box 801, Nashville, TN 37202
615/749-6113

(JOW) Joint Office of Worship, 1044 Alta Vista Road, Louisville, KY 40205.

(MDS) Materials Distribution Service, 341 Ponce de Leon Avenue, N.E., Atlanta, GA 30365.

ACKNOWLEDGMENTS

Material from the following sources is acknowledged and is used by permission. Adaptations are by permission of copyright holders.

Scripture quotations from the Revised Standard Version of the Bible are copyrighted 1946, 1952, © 1971, 1973 by the Division of Christian Education of the National Council of the Churches of Christ in the U.S.A.

Scripture quotations from The New English Bible are copyrighted © 1961, 1970 by The Delegates of the Oxford University Press and The Syndics of the Cambridge University Press.

Scripture quotations from The Bible in Today's English Version are copyrighted © 1976 by the American Bible Society.

"Lord, have mercy" (83, 84, 86), "Glory to God in the highest" (92), the Nicene Creed (135), the Apostles' Creed (136), the preface dialogue (183–189, 197, 198), "Holy, holy, holy Lord" (183–189, 191, 192), the Lord's Prayer (207), "Jesus, Lamb of God" (212, 213), "Lord, now you let your servant go in peace" (229), are from *Prayers We Have in Common*, copyright © 1970, 1971, and 1975 by International Consultation on English Texts.

The Book of Common Worship, copyright © 1932 and 1946 by The Board of Christian Education of the Presbyterian Church in the United States of America. Used by permission of The Westminster Press.

Service for the Lord's Day and Lectionary for the Christian Year, copyright © MCMLXIV by W. L. Jenkins. Used by permission of The Westminster Press.

The Book of Common Worship, Provisional Services, copyright © MCMLXVI by W. L. Jenkins. Used by permission of The Westminster Press.

The Worshipbook—Services, copyright © MCMLXX by The Westminster Press.

The Book of Common Prayer, copyright © 1977 by Charles Mortimer Guilbert as Custodian of the Standard Book of Common Prayer.

Lutheran Book of Worship, copyright © 1978 by Lutheran Church in America, The American Lutheran Church, The Evangelical Lutheran Church of Canada, and The Lutheran Church—Missouri Synod. Used by permission of Augsburg Publishing House.

Excerpts from the English translation of *The Roman Missal* © 1973, International Committee on English in the Liturgy, Inc. All rights reserved. Altered with permission.

We Gather Together, copyright © 1972, 1976, 1979, 1980 by The United Methodist Publishing House.

General Services, copyright © 1984 by The United Methodist Publishing House.

Great Prayer of Thanksgiving D (186) is adapted from *Eucharistic Prayer of Hippolytus: Text for Consultation*, copyright © 1983 International Committee on English in the Liturgy, Inc.

Great Prayer of Thanksgiving E (187) is copyright © 1975 by Marion J. Hatchett, Chairman, The Committee on a Common Eucharistic Prayer.

Great Prayer of Thanksgiving F (188) is from *The Sacrament of the Lord's Supper: A New Text 1984*, copyright © 1984 by Consultation on Church Union.

A Book of Services of The United Reformed Church in England and Wales, copyright © 1980 by The Saint Andrew Press.

The Alternative Service Book 1980, copyright © 1980 by The Central Board of Finance of the Church of England

An Australian Prayer Book, copyright © 1978 by The Church of England in Australia

Uniting Church Worship Services: Holy Communion, copyright © 1980 by The Uniting Church in Australia Assembly Commission on Liturgy.

Service Book, copyright © 1969 by the United Church of Canada.

Extracts from the *Book of Common Prayer* of 1662, which is Crown Copyright in England, are reproduced by permission of Eyre & Spottiswoode, Her Majesty's Printers